A GUIDE TO BUILDING AND MANAGING A COMMERCIAL PROPERTY PORTFOLIO
THE EASYWAY

STEVEN RIMMER

Editor: Roger Sproston

Easyway Guides

Easyway Guides

© Straightforward Co Ltd 2023

All rights reserved. No part of this publication may be reproduced in a retrieval system or transmitted by any means, electronic or mechanical, photocopying or otherwise, without the prior permission of the copyright holders.

ISBN

978-1-80236-168-1

Printed by 4Edge Press www.4Edge.co.uk

Cover design by BW Studio Derby

Whilst every effort has been made to ensure that the information contained within this book is correct at the time of going to press, the author and publisher can take no responsibility for the errors or omissions contained within.

Contents

Introduction

Part 1. Building Up Your Commercial Property Portfolio-An Overview

Chapter 1. The Commercial Property Market	11
Chapter 2. The Main Characteristics of Commercial Properties	17
Chapter 3. Buying Commercial Property	21
Chapter 4. Commercial Property Funds and Self-Invested Personal Pension Schemes	35
Chapter 5. Tax and Commercial Property	45
Chapter 6. Commercial Property and the Planning System	53
Chapter 7. Purchasing a Commercial Property at Auction	67

Part 2. For the Smaller Investor: Managing Your Commercial Property Portfolio-General Advice.

Chapter 8. Business Leases Generally	87
Chapter 9. Service Charges and Business Leases	101
Chapter 10. Assignment and Sub-Letting of Business Leases	109
Chapter 11. Repossession of a Business Lease	111

Chapter 12. Business Leases and Disputes   115

Chapter 13. Security of Tenure for Business tenants   119

Conclusion   133

Useful Addresses and Websites

Index

Appendix 1. Forms and their purposes under the Landlord and Tenant Act 1954 Part 2

Appendix 2. Sample Business Lease

****

Introduction

A Guide to Building and Managing a Commercial Property Portfolio - The Easyway, **updated to 2023**, has been written specifically for the smaller investor who wishes to invest in commercial property and develop a portfolio of properties which will produce an income and also, over time, enhanced capital value. It is also for those who wish to develop a mixed portfolio of directly owned properties and investments through property funds.

Commercial property investment, whether through commercial property funds or through direct investment in smaller retail units or office blocks, has been a bit of a roller coaster. Like every or asset class, this particular investment has suffered due to the advent of the Coronavirus. This relates to the move to working from home, as a necessity of social distancing. Now, more and more people are returning to work and the demand for office space is picking up. In short, the sector is starting to pick up and careful investment can produce good returns.

However, saying that, we are now, in 2023, in a period of economic uncertainty and more and more businesses are collapsing, or going into voluntary administration, once again disrupting the supply and demand balance in the world of commercial property

The situation that has existed for a few years now is that tenants of commercial property are putting owners in a position where they must accept reduced rents. It is very important indeed when considering investing in commercial property, to consider all the variables before making that decision.

Commercial property is different to residential property as, although the legal structure of ownership is the same, different rules apply when calculating rental yields and capital values. Also, a different tax regime applies. Different rules also apply to the lease and rent reviews. It is important to know the finer points of commercial investment and management differentiates it from residential investment.

New rules on Energy Performance
One factor that all landlords and would be landlords need to watch out for is that of changing rules on Energy performance of Office space. Tough energy rules mean landlords must rebuild their sites or leave them empty.

From April 1, 2023, landlords will be forbidden from striking new leases with commercial tenants unless their buildings meet tough new energy standards. The move threatens to further grind down owners of office buildings who have already been battered by the working-from-home revolution. Up to 24,000 offices in England have yet to meet the new energy standards, according to Estates Gazette, the news and analysis provider for the commercial property sector. From next year, offices will need to hold a minimum "E" rates energy performance certificate (EPC). In 2027, the bar rises to "C" – and it goes up to "B" in 2030, when more than 63,000 offices that have more than 400 million sq ft of space – about 800 skyscrapers the size of London's famous Gherkin – will have to improve their energy efficiency or close their doors. London is the worst hit by the new regulations A survey by the Swedish

Introduction

bank Handels banken found that a quarter of landlords were unaware of the timetable, which many feel is horribly tight.

Faced by the new rules, developers owning draughty, thin-walled old office blocks from the 1970s or eighties are knocking them down and redeveloping sites with "zero-carbon" building methods, such as reusing steel. "Developers understand the need to cut carbon," said Melanie Leech, head of the British Property Federation. "The market is driving action ahead of any legislation. The smart ones have figured out that there are massive opportunities for early adopters." Some believe that developers will overhaul existing buildings rather than replace them outright. That may not always be their choice. Critics argue retrofitting existing buildings produce less environmental damage than knocking them down and rebuilding them,

*

In Part 1, this book will initially concentrate on commercial property investment generally, defining commercial property and discussing issues such as costs of investing and the various ways that an individual can invest. We will also discuss the economics of investing and the tax regime. Following this we will discuss acquisition of commercial property through an auction, which is becoming increasing popular, with bargains to be found.

In Part 2 of the book, we will be discussing the areas which a small investor needs to understand if they are thinking of going it alone and, for example, investing in smaller retail units such as shops and offices. These areas encompass the nature of a business lease, legal ownership, rent reviews and the rights of landlord and tenant, service charges and repairs and maintenance. In addition, we will discuss the landlords right to repossess commercial property.

The book is wide ranging, designed to appeal to the smaller investor and highlights all the relevant areas relating to property investment and ongoing management.

Steven Rimmer.

BUILDING UP YOUR COMMERCIAL PROPERTY PORTFOLIO

Chapter 1

The Commercial Property Market-an Overview

Until relatively recently, the commercial property market has been the domain of the larger investor, such as institutional investors (pension funds for example) and professional investors. This is because of the high capital outlay required and the levels of expertise needed. However, things have changed somewhat in the last few years and more and more individual investors are getting involved. This book, although outlining property funds and other funds which enable smaller investors to get involved in larger projects, also refers to the purchase of smaller units such as office blocks and retail shops which can be bought and managed by individuals.

There is about £860 billion of commercial property in the UK. This is far less than the overall value of residential property but still very significant, nonetheless. The core sectors of commercial property, shops, offices and industrial units account for most of the market, about 80%. Around half of this is investment property which is rented to tenants by landlords. The remainder is mostly owned by occupiers, mainly private companies and public sector and non-profit organisations.

Private investors

In the main, readers of this book will be those who are interested in investing privately in commercial property. Because commercial units require large amounts of capital, apart from smaller shops and offices, most private investment has been in residential buy-to-let. However, this has changed somewhat in the last few years and several different types of investment vehicles have emerged which enable the private investor to invest in commercial property. We will be discussing these further on in this book.

Property types

The three principal sectors of the commercial investment market are:

- Retail (shopping centres, retail warehouses, standard shops, supermarkets and department stores)
- Offices (standard offices and business parks)
- Industrial (standard industrial estates and distribution warehousing, or logistical facilities.

There are also several smaller sectors such as leisure (parks, restaurants, pubs and hotels), student accommodation and healthcare properties. An overview of the main sectors reveals that London and the Southeast have the Lion's share of commercial property investments with retail property being more evenly distributed across regions than offices or industrial. Most towns have retail property of all sizes.

Commercial property-investment potential

Commercial property is an attractive investment proposition. However, it is very important to realise that the commercial property market is markedly different to the residential property market. Residential property investment has boomed in the last few decades as the ability of the smaller private investor to access the market has become easier.

The main difference between the two markets are as follows:

- Tenants in residential properties commit to relatively short leases, which are renewable. The typical tenancy of a residential property is for six months which is then renewable or can run on until brought to an end by landlord or tenant.
- Commercial tenants usually sign long-term contracts, such as for ten years, with rent reviews, usually upwards.
- Commercial tenants are normally liable for repairs to the property, while landlords of residential properties are usually responsible.
- The returns from residential property come from both increase in capital value and also rental yield whilst the main income from commercial property is from rental income.
- Commercial properties, with the exception of standard shops or smaller office blocks, usually cost significantly more to buy, particularly shopping centres or large office buildings.

The attractions of investing in commercial property

Because of the longer lease length, the income from commercial property is more stable than residential property, with the average lease being 10 years for retail property and seven years for industrial property. The yield is relatively high, on average 4.9%. However, in the high-inflation environment in 2023, and the economic instability, this may fluctuate. It is true to say that, until recently, commercial property outperformed other investments such as equities, gilts and cash deposits. This is now not the case. We will be looking at various aspects of financing property and working out returns on investment in chapter 3.

Value can be added to commercial property, as direct ownership gives the investor opportunity to manage their assets actively, either to sustain value or enhance it. Active management can include re-negotiating the lease terms of an existing tenant to increase the value, for example by increasing length of the lease or increasing rent payable. Premises can be refurbished thus increasing the value of the property or the property can be redeveloped for a different use (see chapter 6 on planning regulations).

The risks involved

Although there are a number of attractions there are also risks to be aware of when investing in commercial property. Some of the risks relating to the current state of the economy, have already been outlined. There are other risks which need to be considered before making any decision to buy commercial property. These are outlined below.

Location

As with all property, location, location, location holds true. The siting of a building directly affects its value. A commercial property investment is likely to be held for the longer term and the attractiveness of its location can change over time, for better or worse. Factors that can change the attractiveness of a location can include area regeneration or the building of a large store nearby.

Physical characteristics of the building

The type and use (utility) of the building can affect its value. Type of building refers to what sort of building it is, office or shop. The utility refers to what type of benefits the occupier gets from the building. Things that affect utility are location and quality of the building, quality being affected by the materials used in the construction of the building and its internal layout and specification. The risk factor here is depreciation. Whilst all buildings suffer depreciation, advances in building technology or tenants' requirements might change over time. Also, bear in mind the new rules coming into effect in April 2023, concerning energy performance, as outlined in the overview to this book

Tenants

As we have stated, the value of a building very much depends on the rental income it can produce for its owner. After all, this is one of the main reasons, other than an increase in capital value, for investing. If the credit quality of the tenant deteriorates materially during the period of ownership, so does the value of the investment.

Given that we are in a period of uncertainty, with high inflation affecting business, this factor needs to be considered.

Market risks

These are risks that can, and have, affected all sectors of the property market. As with the economy, commercial property investment goes through cycles: periods of growth leading to oversupply and market weakness, followed by stabilisation, absorption and then growth, which leads to shortage of supply and so on. When and where you invest and what period in the cycle is therefore very important. Take a long look at what you intend to invest in.

In the next chapter, we will look at the main characteristics of commercial property, i.e., the legal status of ownership and the main elements contained within leases such as rent reviews.

****

Chapter 2

The Main Characteristics of Commercial Properties

Outlined below are some of the main features of commercial property.

Freehold property, leasehold property and commonholds
As with residential property, there are three main legal classes of ownership of land and property, freehold, leasehold and commonhold. The freeholder effectively owns all the property-land and structures-in perpetuity. They are free to create leases and let out the whole or part of the property for given periods of time. The interest in land that a freeholder can create is called the lease, and this will form a contract between leaseholder (tenant) and freeholder for a given period although the leaseholder has a statutory right to renew (we will be discussing this in more depth later).

The commonhold is a relatively new form of property ownership. The common parts of a development are owned by a commonhold association and the owners acquire a freehold unit subject to the terms of the commonhold. These, however, are not so common in commercial property investments.

Some leases include break clauses giving the landlord and/or the tenant the option to end the lease before its expiry date. These clauses can significantly affect the value of the property because it will affect stability of income, although a break clause can benefit the landlord enabling them to terminate the lease and make improvements.

Privity of contract

Leases signed before 1st January 1996 are subject to "privity of contract" which means that the original tenant remains responsible for the rent and other commitments for the duration of the lease even after it has been transferred to another tenant. For leases assigned after January 1st, 1996, the situation is different. A tenant who assigns a lease if generally released from any future liability under it. However, landlords are permitted (market practice) to require the outgoing tenant to guarantee the liabilities of the specific person to who the lease is assigned.

Privity of contract is important because the investment value of a property depends in part on the financial strength of a tenant. If a blue-chip tenant assigns a lease to a weaker tenant, then the value of a property overall will be diminished.

Rent reviews

We will be discussing rent reviews later in the book as part of the overview of business leases. In brief, the rent review period is agreed with the landlord and the tenant and is set out in the terms of the lease. The typical rent review period is every five years. The rent review is negotiated between landlord and tenant (or their agents) with the final rent decided by referring to comparable property rents. Once agreed, the tenant is committed to paying this income until the next rent review or termination.

The Main Characteristics of Commercial Properties

UK commercial leases have traditionally provided for "upward only" reviews. This means that the new rent cannot be lower than the tenant is currently paying even if the market rents in the area have fallen below that level. If this is the case, the landlord and tenant will usually agree to maintain the rent at current levels.

If the landlord and tenant cannot agree on a rent they can ask an independent arbitrator (often appointed by the RISC) to decide the matter.

Buying and selling commercial property
Commercial property is sold mainly through private markets although it is also usually the case that auctions will sell off commercial units of one sort or another. Many agents will now also market commercial properties through the internet.

In the next chapter, we will look at the process of purchasing commercial properties, raising finance and the costs of acquisition.

****

Chapter 3

Buying Commercial Property

Buying commercial property isn't, on the face of it, drastically different from residential buy-to-let investment. You find the property, put in an offer and, when it is accepted, go through legal searches and due diligence before exchange and completion. However, it is important to know that there are different forces at play, starting with the matter of sourcing the property.

Most commercial properties are sold through private treaty – the well-trodden route of offer-acceptance-contract. A smaller number are sold at auction – a useful route for those new to the game. At auctions you will find smaller lot sizes which may be more suitable for the smaller investor. See chapter 7 which gives more details of property auctions.

Because the commercial sector is far more insular than the residential sector in terms of advisers and agents, It is best, when you are ready to purchase a property, to take advice from a chartered surveyor with an investment/agency background rather than employing a standard conveyancing solicitor.

Whether you take the auction route (where, if the successful bidder, you will need to hand over 10 per cent on the day and expect completion within a month) or private treaty, you need to have your finance in place.

Sourcing the best lender for you

Not surprisingly, the mortgage market has tightened up in 2023, due to the current inflationary environment.

Like a residential mortgage, you should always search the market for the best possible deal for you. Although the high street is an obvious starting place, they may not have the most competitive deals available. You should actively consider using the services of an impartial, specialist commercial mortgage broker that covers the whole market. A broker will scour the market for the best deal and the most appropriate deal relevant to your business sector. Your broker should then continue to search for the market going forward in order to make sure you are constantly benefiting from the best rates available. You can search for a specialist mortgage broker at the National Association of Commercial Finance Brokers.

Generally, commercial mortgages are for 15 years or more, and, as with a residential mortgage, the premises will be at risk if you are unable to keep up your repayments. Most mainstream lenders offer commercial mortgages, but it's important that you can meet their lending criteria. Although some lenders may still accept applicants or businesses with an adverse credit history, it helps if you can show a clean credit record, as this will give you greater choice and a more competitive deal. Lenders will apply a loan to value ratio to the mortgage and will often require you to invest some of your own money into the property. The more of your own money you invest, the more chance you will have of securing the mortgage.

Some lenders may impose restrictions on the property, such as the ability to sub-let to other businesses, so you should seek professional advice from your solicitor, and if required, a chartered surveyor.

What information will the bank need?

Most lenders will request a lot of commercial information and it is worth preparing this from the start to help your application run smoothly. The information might include documents on the performance of the business.

Remember, the main concerns of any lender will be whether you can afford to repay the loan and, should you default, whether the property is worth enough to cover the value of the loan. Should you be buying a commercial property which has a business integral to it, such as a shop or office, you may need to provide additional information, such as:

- Audited accounts for the last two years
- A profit and loss forecast for the next few years
- Current business performance
- The personal details of the key stakeholders in the business for credit-checking
- Asset and liability statements for each applicant
- A business plan detailing how the property will contribute to your cash flow and how you plan on repaying the loan
- The credit status of the business
- Reasons why the business is being sold
- Details of any personal investments involved
- Growth projections for the business

Repaying the mortgage

The mortgage repayment options are similar to those in the residential mortgage market, although you can expect to pay a slightly higher rate of interest, as commercial mortgages are generally seen as a higher risk to lenders. This is where it helps to have a big deposit, as a deposit of less than 20 per cent may mean you pay a much higher interest rate to offset the increased risk to the lender.

In the commercial mortgage market, most deals are either fixed rate or variable rate. Fixed rate deals are usually between two and five years and can provide you with repayment stability if this is required, although you won't be able to take advantage of any falls in the base rate. On the other hand, taking a variable rate mortgage will allow you to benefit from any reductions in the base rate, but will also mean repayments may increase if the base rate increases.

The specific repayment options available are like those found in the residential mortgage market. A repayment mortgage option (where you pay the capital and interest back each month) means you will have all your bases covered in repaying what you have borrowed. You can also choose an interest-only mortgage, where you only repay the interest back each month on the amount you have borrowed. If you choose this option, the lender will almost certainly seek evidence of an appropriate insurance or investment policy that will cover the outstanding capital at the end of the loan term.

There are additional costs associated with taking out a commercial mortgage and you should take these into account before you embark on your mortgage search or seek clarification from your lender or broker.

Other fees and costs to consider

There are additional costs associated with taking out a commercial mortgage and you should take these into account before you embark on your mortgage search or seek clarification from your lender or broker.

- Arrangement fees (usually between 0.5 per cent and 1.5 per cent of the loan value)
- Valuation fees (the cost of the lender undertaking a survey on the property to establish its value)
- Legal fees (including legal documents, insurance and your own surveys)
- Redemption penalties (a fee payable to the lender if you pay off your mortgage before the agreed term)
- As with any mortgage, you should always seek the appropriate professional and legal advice before taking out a commercial mortgage.

Buying costs

Buying costs for commercial property will amount to around 5.8 per cent – the bulk of that on stamp duty. See table below. Estate agents will charge buyers 1 per cent plus VAT and the solicitor typically 0.5 per cent plus VAT. The current Stamp Duty Land Tax rates (2023-2024) are:

(overleaf)

Non-residential and mixed-use land and property rates

You pay SDLT on increasing portions of the property price (or 'consideration') when you pay £150,000 or more for non-residential or mixed-use land or property. You must still send an SDLT return for most transactions under £150,000.

Non-residential property includes:
- commercial property, e.g., shops or offices
- agricultural land
- forests
- any other land or property which is not used as a residence
- 6 or more residential properties bought in a single transaction

A 'mixed use' property is one that has both residential and non-residential elements, e.g., a flat connected to a shop, doctor's surgery or office.

Freehold sales and transfers

You can also use this table over leaf to work out the SDLT rate for a lease premium.

Property or lease premium or transfer value	SDLT rate
Up to £150,000	Zero
The next £100,000 (the portion from £150,001 to £250,000)	2%
The remaining amount (the portion above £250,000)	5%

Example If you buy a freehold commercial property for £275,000, the SDLT you owe is calculated as follows:
- 0% on the first £150,000 = £0
- 2% on the next £100,000 = £2,000
- 5% on the final £25,000 = £1,250
- Total SDLT = £3,250

New leasehold sales and transfers

When you buy a new non-residential or mixed use leasehold you pay SDLT on both the:

- purchase price of the lease (the 'lease premium') using the rates above
- value of the annual rent you pay (the 'net present value')

These are calculated separately then added together.

If you buy an existing ('assigned') lease, you only pay SDLT on the lease price (or 'consideration'). The net present value (NPV) is based on the total rent over the life of the lease. You don't pay SDLT on the rent if the NPV is less than £150,000.

Net present value of rent	SDLT rate
£0 to £150,000	Zero
The portion from £150,001 to £5,000,000	1%

Net present value of rent	SDLT rate
The portion above £5,000,000	2%

How much you'll pay
You can work out how much SDLT you'll pay for your non-residential lease using HM Revenue and Customs' (HMRC) SDLT calculator. You may pay a higher rate of SDLT for multiple purchases or transfers from the same seller.

SDLT relief's
Some transactions may qualify for relief, which can reduce the amount of tax payable, SDLT relief can be claimed online. Relief may be claimed when companies within the same group buy or sell to/from each other within the following criteria:
- Both parties are companies
- Both companies are members of the same group at the date of transaction

Charities are able to claim SDLT relief from the point when they purchase property or land for charitable purposes. The relief can be discontinued within the three years of the transaction if the property reverts from being used for charitable purposes.

Additional costs
These can include drafting the lease as, unlike Assured shorthold tenancy agreements (ASTs) in residential property, there is no

standard format for commercial properties. Each new lease drafted is bespoke to the particular property and parties involved, so drafting it can cost four times that of a residential lease.

It is also recommended that you factor the cost of empty business rates into any price valuation along with your normal letting void risks. Once a lease ends, the landlord has a three-month exemption before paying these rates, which are instead of council tax and generally reflect about a third of the property's annual rental income – unless you buy a listed commercial property, which would be exempt.

Another essential expense is a building survey. Employing a specialist building surveyor is essential when you make the leap from residential to commercial investment. Your surveyor may also advise getting an environmental report, particularly for industrial sites or properties you may redevelop in the future. Most commercial property investment usually comes with a tenant in situ. The alternative – buying an empty property and letting it yourself – is higher risk and best suited to more sophisticated investors. With an already tenanted property, the rent is fixed and you're paid in advance quarterly, with rent reviews only upward, not downwards, so you can budget for your costs in advance.

Commercial property transactions tend to go through more quickly than residential ones – particularly as there are no chains – so completion in a couple of months is standard. If the process is drawn out, it's usually because of doubts over the tenant. A big part of the value of the property depends on who your tenant is and how good they are – and you pay a considerable amount more for a tenant who will pose you less risk.

The return on your investment-valuation of commercial property and property yields

There is one key principle associated with the process of investing in commercial property that needs to be understood, and that it is the subject of property yield, or return on investment (ROI). Return on investment or property yield is one of the most critical components of the entire property investment process and thankfully, working it out involves a straightforward calculation. Put simply, yield is known as the annual return on your capital investment and is usually expressed as a percentage of the capital value.

Gross & Net Yield

At an introductory level there are two forms of yield for an investor to consider; net yield and gross yield. Gross yield is calculated by dividing a property's annual rental income by the building's value; whilst net yield is determined by first subtracting the property's yearly operational costs from its annual rent and then dividing this by the building's value.

Gross Yield = Annual Rent / Property Value

Net Yield = (Annual Rent - Operational Costs) / Property Value

All Risks Yield

Investors should also be aware of what is known as an "all risks yield". All risks yield is important if you are investing in commercial property, as this form of yield is the amount that Chartered surveyors, and valuation professionals will utilise to showcase the risks associated with certain investments. Generally, in order to determine an all risks yield figure and understand how it is compiled, you should always bear in mind a few rules as this will help you to understand the basic concepts behind the figures.

The first thing to understand is that in a buoyant property market property yields are likely to fall. This occurs because the overall capital value of property increases with market demand whilst the annual rent is likely to remain static (until review) at a lower percentage of the total capital value. Conversely however, in a falling property market, yields will increase.

Property Yield versus Capital Value
Many property investors often question why more emphasis is placed on property yield or return as opposed to overall capital values. The answer to this is straightforward. Capital values can only really be generated by reviewing recent, comparable transactions of similar properties in similar locations. Yield, however, is easily compared across a platform of properties.

Because of this, it is common practice to apply a percentage yield figure as a multiplier against a property's annual rental income, as this will help to build an estimate of the capital value of the property.

Calculate Property Values Using Yields
If a commercial property is being let, for say one hundred and fifty thousand pounds per annum, and an approximate yield across nearly identical properties is identified at around 6 per cent, this would mean that the capital value of the property will be the result of one hundred and fifty thousand divided by 6, multiplied by one hundred.

Capital Value = (Annual Rental Income / Yield) x 100
In this example:
Annual Rental Income = £150,000
Yield = 6%
Capital Value = (£150,000 / 6) x 100

Capital Value = £2.5 Million

Covenant Strength
Investors should also be aware that property yield figures can also be "manipulated" to show alternative capital values that more accurately reflect investment risk. This way the investor risk associated with the renting out of a property can be taken in to account more fully.

For instance, if a tenant is known to be reliable, has a good reputation and is financially very strong, then this will mean that they will present a lower level of risk to the property owner, which will, in turn, means that the value of the tenanted property will be higher to a prospective investor. Lease strength of this nature is commonly referred to as "covenant strength" and is a term used in the property world to denote the strength or quality of a commercial tenant. A FTSE 100 company would be viewed as a very strong tenant, much more likely to keep to its lease covenants, to pay its rent on time and not to break any of its lease obligations. On the flip side however, if a company that wishes to let a commercial property poses a threat of missed rental payments, broken obligations and the like, then this obviously increases investor risk and the investment value of the tenanted property will be affected accordingly, resulting in a less favourable yield.

****

Chapter 4

Commercial Property Investment-Commercial Property Funds and SIPP'S

It is likely that the person who wishes to build up a commercial property portfolio will do so through two mediums: through the acquisition of interests in property through investment companies and shares or through Self Investment Personal Pension Schemes-this route is less hands on but provides return on your investment; through a direct acquisition such as a small office block or a commercial premises such as a shop or industrial unit. This chapter deals with the first route.

Commercial property funds allow small investors to become part owners of huge properties. There are two different types of commercial property funds within which you can invest. They both come with different benefits and risks.

Direct or 'bricks and mortar' commercial property funds
Bricks and mortar funds refer to direct commercial property investment, meaning that actual physical properties are bought by the fund. Risk is spread across several different properties and, therefore, if one property is not occupied (and therefore earning no income from rent), others within the fund can generate income. Your returns come from a combination of increased value of the

properties in the fund and, more importantly, the rental income. Rental income provides you with an annual return, and when you cash in your investment, you'll hopefully receive the sum you initially invested, plus any growth in value of the properties within the fund.

Benefits and risks of direct commercial property investment funds
With direct property funds, rental income can be relatively secure in comparison to other asset classes because of factors like long lease lengths (typically five years or more), less risk of default than residential properties and upward-only rent reviews, meaning that rental income increases by at least inflation each year. You also don't have the hassle of property management, which falls to the manager of your fund. It's the manager's responsibility to source tenants, invest in property in prime locations and negotiate lease lengths.

A major downside of direct investment, however, is that property markets are highly illiquid compared to most other financial markets, meaning that buying or selling property can take months, and can make it difficult to sell your holding in the fund quickly.

Beware the lock-out of direct commercial property investment funds
When the (major) financial crisis rocked the economy in 2008, many direct property fund investors found they could not take their money out as property values plunged. (Oddly enough, this is now being repeated in 2023). This was because property funds have a

little known clause that allows fund managers to shut off payments to investors wanting to exit the funds if there are "exceptional circumstances."

Under Financial Conduct Authority rules, property funds can suspend trading for 28 days while they try to raise enough cash by selling properties to meet the repayments of investors looking to reclaim their cash. This 28-day period can recur until the fund has enough capital to meet its obligations.

Fund managers argued this was for the benefit of investors, as a fire-sale of properties in such conditions would mean they would not be able to realise their full value.

Indirect commercial property funds.
These funds, usually in the form of unit trusts and OEICS (Open Ended Investment Companies), buy shares in companies that invest in property. These shares are listed on the Stock Exchange and traded on a daily basis and, therefore, don't have the liquidity problems of direct commercial property funds, meaning you can move in and out of the fund freely.

Returns are gained like any other investment in shares, through share price appreciation and dividend income, rather than directly through property price increases and rental income. But while you get the benefit of the liquidity of an equity-like product, you also get the volatility of investing on the stock market.

The great majority (over 80%) of these property companies are known as Real Estate Investment Trusts (REITs) and have greater tax benefits than other listed property companies. REIT companies don't pay corporation tax on their assets, on the condition that 90%

of profits are paid to shareholders as dividends, which in turn could mean higher payouts. REIT investors pay either 20% or 40% tax, because they're classed as property-letting income.

To qualify for their special tax status, a UK REIT must meet certain conditions:

- It must be a UK tax resident
- It must be listed on a recognised stock exchange, with the shares widely held
- It must not be an open ended company

A REIT must also hold at least three investment properties, though the definition of investment property includes three separate rental units within one building. No single property may represent more than 40% of the total portfolio value. There are a number of other rules and regulations surrounding REIT's and taxation which can be obtained from HMRC.

Other ways to invest in commercial property
Property investment trusts

Alternatively, you could invest in property investment trusts, which will pool your money to buy property and property company shares. The difference between these and REITs is that they're considered to be like any other company, so tax on dividends is only 8.75% for basic-rate payers and 33.75% for higher-rate payers. Investment trusts can do things that unit trusts and OEICS can't. For example, many property investment trusts use gearing - a process whereby the companies borrow money - to boost the amount they can put into property beyond what you have invested. While this can enhance gains in a rising market, it can magnify losses if returns fall.

Self-Invested Personal Pension Plan (SIPP)

Investing in commercial property through your SIPP, if you have one, offers many advantages that include:
- tax relief on contributions paid into your SIPP.
- exemption from capital gains tax when the property is sold.
- exemption from income tax on any rental payments.
- increased cash flow if property is purchased from you or your company.

Any property purchased by your SIPP will normally be held in an individual sub-trust established under the principal pension trust deed. You and the Trustees will be appointed as the trustees of the sub-trust, which will purchase the property. This means that the property is legally owned by the trustees of the sub-trust and registered with the Land Registry in the names of the trustees, which includes you. By using this method of purchase, the sub-trust empowers you to take control of the management of the property. Some SIPP operators will insist on you appointing a specific property management company.

When considering the type of property you wish to invest in, there are many things that you must take into account. Pensions legislation restricts you from investing in most types of residential property, or any other property where you would be able to gain some form of personal benefit. Most types of commercial property and land are acceptable, but care must be taken to ensure that any

risks associated with the purchase are carefully managed. You can consider the purchase of commercial property or land from any party, including connected parties. All property purchases and any lease arrangements must be on a fully commercial basis at arm's length. A connected party is:
- you.
- your spouse, civil partner or relative.
- a relative of your spouse or civil partner.
- a business partner, their spouse or civil partner.
- a company connected with you, your spouse or civil partner.
- the trustee(s) of a settlement for which you are a settler, or for which a person who is still alive and connected to you is a settlor.

Acceptable property for investment through a SIPP
- Commercial property or land of any kind, usually leased back to a connected or third party.
- Hotels, prisons, care homes and public houses, provided they meet appropriate pensions
- Forestry, woodland and agricultural land, provided there is no residential element included.

In addition, HMRC may investigate any fishing or hunting rights, or any other leisure or recreational activities on the land, to ensure you, or anyone connected to you, could not directly benefit from these activities following the acquisition of the land by your SIPP, without paying the appropriate market rate for the activity.

Overseas commercial property is acceptable, provided it meets the criteria applicable to the purchase of any property in the UK, including ensuring title can be identified and any risk issues can be resolved. Any foreign documents associated with the property must be accompanied by English translations. You will need to appoint a lawyer qualified in the appropriate jurisdiction to act on behalf of your SIPP.

Overseas hotel rooms may be acceptable provided they meet appropriate HMRC requirements.

Land for development

This could be commercial or residential. The following points need to be considered before investing in land for development.

- If it is intended that the land is to be developed by a connected party, you will need to obtain independent quotations from three different contractors, including the connected party. This is to ensure the work is carried out on a fully commercial basis at arm's length. Architect's certificates for partially completed and fully completed development work may also be required.
- How your SIPP will fund the cost of the work. The work must be carried out for the benefit of the SIPP. In general, it should enhance the value of the property and subsequently enhance the potential benefits from your SIPP. If residential property is being developed, it must be sold prior to becoming suitable for use as a dwelling.
- Frequent purchases and sales may be considered as trading by HMRC and consequently assessable to tax.

Prohibited property

All residential property is prohibited, even if planning consent has been granted for a change of use to commercial. Only when the change of use has been completed is your SIPP able to purchase the property. A freehold commercial property, which contains a residential element, such as a flat on a long residential lease, with a nominal ground rent, is still considered by HMRC to be a residential property. In these circumstances it is only possible to proceed with a purchase if the vendor is prepared to sell only the commercial part to your SIPP. For example, by granting a long leasehold interest in the commercial premises. There are exceptions to this regulation, which are:

- residential property, which is occupied by an employee, as a condition of employment, who is not connected with his or her employer or connected to you, for example a caretaker
- residential property, which is occupied by a person other than you (or a person connected with you), in connection with that person's occupation of the business premises, for example a shop with an integral flat above.

Once you have identified a suitable property investment, the next stage is to consider how the purchase will be funded, as contracts for purchase cannot be exchanged until the funding is in place. Contributions, which can be made into your SIPP, are unlimited. There is, however, a limit on the level of contributions eligible for tax relief in any one tax year, known as the annual allowance. There is also a limit on the funds you may have in your SIPP when you take your benefits, known as the lifetime allowance. Funds in excess of the lifetime allowance will be subject to additional tax charges unless you have obtained the necessary pension protection.

You may obtain tax relief in excess of the annual allowance in a single tax year by using unused annual allowance from the previous three qualifying tax years, provided you were a member of a UK registered pension scheme. This facility is called carry-forward.

Borrowing money

Your SIPP can borrow money to help fund the purchase. The borrowing can be from any source, usually a bank, but you may also borrow from a connected party, provided it is on a fully commercial basis, subject to a commercial rate of interest and is formally documented with all parties signing the agreement. In most cases trustees would expect borrowing repayments to be met from the rental income. Pensions legislation requirements limit your SIPP's total borrowing to 50% of its net fund value at the time the loan is drawn down. The net fund value excludes any existing borrowing. Any existing SIPP borrowing will be deducted to calculate the net value of your SIPP. The 50% borrowing limit will take into account any existing outstanding borrowing already in place.

It may be possible for your SIPP to apply for a grant to help purchase and develop a property, for example, when the area the property is in is part of a redevelopment program. A grant may be an attractive proposition, but there are certain considerations to take into account before proceeding.

- The grant is treated as a donation to the SIPP and must not result in the SIPP exceeding the total lifetime allowance.

- The body making the grant available must be happy to make it available to the SIPP.
- The terms and conditions attached to the grant must not impose any onerous covenants, such as a requirement to provide employment or impose any selling restrictions. The terms of any claw-back of the grant should also be carefully considered in the event of the disposal.

****

Chapter 5

Tax and Commercial Property

In a UK taxation context, there are several key differences between the treatment of commercial and residential property. Commercial property has several tax advantages not available to most residential property investors, including capital allowances, superior taper relief on capital gains and the ability to use pension funds for investment.

Commercial property makes a good target for taxation. Its location is static, its ownership documented, and the commercial property tax liability can be calculated with more certainty. Below are the main taxation factors that should be considered when buying, renting and disposing of property:

Purchasing a commercial property

VAT exemption on commercial property
As a general rule, the sale or lease of a commercial property is exempt from VAT, which means neither a purchaser nor a tenant would have to pay VAT. That exemption extends to the exchange of interests in, rights over or licences to occupy commercial properties. While that may be good news for a purchaser, it does mean that when a vendor or landlord supplies a property that is exempt from VAT, they are unable to recover any VAT incurred on related costs.

And there are certain exceptions to this rule. VAT at the standard rate is applied to commercial property transactions where the property involved is new, i.e., less than 3 years old, or where the vendor or landlord has elected to charge VAT. The latter may occur where a property has been refurbished or renovated, and the vendor or landlord is looking to recover the VAT costs associated with that work.

Electing to charge VAT
Commercial property owners can opt to charge VAT at the standard rate (currently 20%) when selling or leasing their property. If they do so, they must charge VAT on all supplies they make relating to that property – but they are also then able to recover VAT charged to them on any costs related to the property. If a supplier wishes to charge VAT on a commercial property transaction, there are certain restrictions and procedures that they must comply with.

The supplier must decide to opt to tax the property and notify HMRC of their intentions in writing within 30 days of this decision. It is important that the decision to opt is taken before any exempt supplies are made in respect of the property. If the supplier has previously made exempt supplies in respect of a particular property or piece of land, they will need to get permission from HMRC if they wish to elect to charge VAT on future supplies in relation to that land/building. Once a supplier has notified HMRC of their option to tax, that decision lasts for 20 years and is largely regarded as irrevocable, so making the right long-term decision is crucial. It should be noted that the option to charge VAT does not follow the property, so the next purchaser or tenant will need to decide whether to opt to tax and this will depend on their use of the building. One issue to consider is the potential market for the property itself. If the market sector is likely to include significant numbers of buyers who themselves cannot recover VAT as they make exempt supplies– such as banks, financial institutions, and businesses in the health, welfare and charitable sectors – electing to charge VAT can have a negative impact on the ability to sell or lease a property.

Transfer of a going concern
If the property being sold is capable of being run as a property rental business (for example, being sold with tenants in place or with the benefit of an existing lease), and the buyer intends to carry on the same type of business, this commercial property transaction may then be classed as a Transfer of Going Concern (TOGC).

A TOGC is outside of the scope of VAT, and so no VAT will be payable – which could be an attractive option for buyers in these circumstances. For the TOGC conditions to be met, the buyer must mirror the seller's VAT position by the date of transfer. This means that if the seller is registered for VAT and has opted to tax the building, the buyer must do likewise and the notification of the option to tax must be received by HMRC by the date of transfer.

VAT on the sale of new commercial property
The sale of a 'new' commercial property – i.e., a property that is less than three years old – will be liable to VAT at the standard rate. In these situations, the buyer of a new commercial property who intends to rent it out is likely to elect to charge VAT on rents going

forward and on a future sale of the property (unless it qualifies as a TOGC) in order to recover the VAT charged on an acquisition.

- *Stamp Duty Land Tax (SDLT)*: SDLT is applicable if the commercial property is situated in England, Wales, or Northern Ireland. SDLT on commercial property starts at 2% for transactions over £150,000 and increases (on a 'slice' basis) to 5% for transactions over £250,000. The same rates of SDLT apply to individual, trustee and corporate purchasers. SDLT applies to the VAT inclusive transaction value, where VAT is payable.
- *Land & Buildings Transaction Tax (LBTT) and Land Transaction Tax (LTT)*: LBTT is applicable if the commercial property is situated in Scotland and in addition, from 1 April 2018, SDLT was replaced in Wales by a devolved LTT. In more general terms, LBTT and LTT are both very similar to SDLT however the administrations are not alike.
- *Other considerations on purchase of commercial property*: A purchaser must review the capital allowances position and consider making a section 198 election. Also, they must consider the VAT position of the property and whether VAT will be payable on its acquisition or whether the property can be transferred as a VAT exempt 'transfer of a going concern' (TOGC). This depends on whether the sellers have opted to tax for VAT purposes; this may, in part, depend on whether their tenants are able to recover any VAT charged on rents. To qualify for TOGC treatment, the purchaser will need to register for VAT.
- It is worth nothing that in case of shares in a company owning commercial property are purchased, compared to the property

itself, no SDLT is applicable. Rather, a stamp duty of 0.5% is payable on the consideration given for shares in a UK company.

Renting out the commercial property

Income from let commercial property is subjected to tax. Deductions are available for revenue expenses, such as interest and letting agents' fees. The tax rates applicable depend on whether the lessor is an individual, trust, or company. A good guide to current rates can be obtained at:

https://www.mfsuk.com/blog/commercial-property-tax-guide/

Commercial property tax for non-UK investors

The UK tax regime applicable to non-UK investors in commercial property has, in the past, been generous. The transaction tax on a commercial property acquisition is low and so is the effective rate of tax on gains realised on the disposal of the commercial property.

Most UK commercial property ventures exist with a non-UK company acting as a special purpose vehicle. This is a tax efficient way out that offers options in terms of future disposal routes when an investor wants to exit the investment. Investment into a UK commercial property through a non-UK company removes the possibility of any applicability of UK inheritance tax.

Ownership of UK commercial property: inheritance tax

UK inheritance tax (IHT) is applicable to UK assets which are directly owned, regardless of the residence or domicile status of the owner of the commercial property. IHT is liable to tax on death at 40% in relation to assets held at death. IHT is also applicable to any gifts made within seven years prior to death, though there is a narrowing of the IHT rate.

Transfers of commercial property into trust will attract a 20% IHT charge and the UK assets will roughly be subject to a 6% IHT charge every 10 years, with a pro-rated 6% IHT charge on any distributions from the trust. Where the settlor of the trust retains an interest in the trust, in addition to these charges, the property will remain in their estate for IHT purposes.

Tax relief: An individual who is not domiciled in the UK and is not considered to be domiciled in the UK can shelter the value of the commercial property from IHT by owning the property through a non-UK resident company. For IHT purposes they are treated as owning the non-UK situs shares.

Sale of commercial property

Commercial property owners may have to pay Capital Gains Tax if they make a profit ('gain') when they sell (or 'dispose of') property that's not your home, for example:

1. buy-to-let properties
2. business premises
3. land
4. inherited property

Commercial property owners do not usually need to pay tax on gifts to your husband, wife, civil partner or a charity. They may get tax relief if the commercial property is a business asset.

If the commercial property was occupied by a dependent relative, they may not have to pay.

- *Residence*: Traditionally, non-residents – individuals, trustees and companies, have not been subject to UK tax on the disposal of commercial property held for investment purposes. Specific rules apply where a property is or becomes a development property. The UK government announced that the position has changed from April 2019. From April 2019, all disposals of UK property by non-residents became subject to capital gains tax (CGT), and the disposals of indirect interests in such commercial property. Gains on commercial property and indirect interests in all types of property has been rebased to April 2019, so that only the element of gain accruing from that date is taxable. Tax is due at the same rate as an equivalent disposal by a UK resident.
- *Individuals*: UK resident individuals are subject to CGT on gains realised on the disposal of UK commercial property at 10% or 20%, depending on whether the individual has any basic rate band remaining after calculating their income for income tax purposes.
- *Trustees*: UK resident trustees are subject to CGT at 20% on gains realised on disposal.
- *Company*: A UK resident company is subject to corporation tax at 19%, increasing to 25% from 1 April 2023, on gains realised on the disposal of commercial property.
- *Recording*: From 6 April 2019 a return needed to be filed within 30 days in relation to any disposal of UK commercial property by a non-UK tax resident. The payment date for any tax due is also 30 days following the date of disposal.

Chapter 6

Commercial Properties and the Planning System

Whether you are buying or leasing a commercial property, you may need to seek permission to use the building for a different purpose than it was originally intended. Many local authorities now have online planning portals that allow you to find the planning history for a building. Building purposes are categorised into "use classes"; if the new purpose falls into the same use class as the existing purpose, you may not need to apply for planning permission.

You should seek advice from a property professional on whether you will need to apply for permission to change the use of your commercial property, and how likely it is that permission will be granted.

Applying for planning permission

Planning permission should be sought from the local planning authority, using the appropriate forms which should be available to download from their website. You will have to pay a fee when you submit the application; the amount will depend on what type of planning permission you are applying for. You will also need properly prepared plans drawn up for the application.

Submitting a planning application

Anyone can apply for planning permission, regardless of who owns the relevant land or buildings, although the legal owner of the site must be formally notified of the plans. You can apply for planning permission yourself, or if the application looks to be quite complex or contentious, you can enlist a chartered surveyor, architect, planning consultant or other appropriate professional to handle the application on your behalf.

It always helps to have an informal discussion with someone at your local planning authority before you go ahead with your application, especially in complex cases. However, you should not take their advice as gospel; planning committees can choose to overrule their suggestions.

Applying for outline or full planning permission

Outline planning permission is applicable to new builds and will only tell you whether a proposal would be accepted in principle, without having to submit more detailed plans. Full planning permission requires all aspects of the proposal to be submitted, including detailed drawings of the new build. Full planning permission can be sought by those who wish to save time, or those who have already been advised that their proposals are likely to be accepted. If the principle of development is unlikely to be an issue or the applicant proposes to carry out the development it is more cost effective and saves time overall to submit a full planning application in the first instance. However, when a landowner will be selling the site, it is more difficult to justify the expense of a full application.

After the application is submitted

When you submit your application, you will be advised that a decision will be made within eight weeks of the application being formally received by the local planning authority, although it may take considerably longer than this.

The local authority may grant permission subject to conditions. These will commonly be in relation to:
- Details that need to be confirmed before the permission can be implemented, known as 'pre-commencement conditions'. For example, approval of the materials to be used.
- Restrictions on the work needed to implement the permission. For example, the hours in which vehicles can access the construction site.
- Restrictions on the use or operation of the development once complete. For example, any subsequent change-of-use.

The authority must give reasons for the conditions when a decision is issued.

The local authority may, as a pre-condition to granting of the planning permission, impose planning obligations, also known as section 106 agreements (based on that section of the 1990 Town & Country Planning Act). These are private agreements made between local authorities and developers and can be attached to a planning permission to make acceptable development which would otherwise be unacceptable in planning terms. The land itself, rather than the person or organisation that develops the land, is bound by a section 106 agreement, something any future owners will need to consider.

Once a decision has been reached, you will receive a document which tells you whether or not your application has been approved, along with an explanation of the committee's reasons if your application has been refused. If permission is granted, the permission will specify how soon the development must begin and how any conditions are to be addressed.

The Community Infrastructure Levy (CIL

The Community Infrastructure Levy (CIL) is a planning charge, introduced by the Planning Act 2008 as a tool for local authorities in England and Wales to help deliver infrastructure to support the development of their area. It came into force on 6 April 2010 through the Community Infrastructure Levy Regulations 2010. Development may be liable for a charge under the CIL if your local planning authority has chosen to set a charge in its area. You will need to enquire with the local authority as to whether they have elected to charge a CIL on developments in their area.

Failure to obtain planning permission, time limits in which the local authority may to take action

If there has been a breach of planning control and the local planning authority (LPA) does not take planning enforcement action within the requisite time periods, then generally the right to do so is lost. The unauthorised development or use becomes lawful and immune from planning enforcement action. Time limits for taking planning enforcement action:

Planning enforcement action must, in general, be taken within either four or ten years, depending on the nature of the breach.

There are, however, some circumstances in which planning enforcement action can be taken outside these time limits.

Four-year rule

No planning enforcement action can be taken after four years where the breach of planning control relates to:

- Building, engineering, mining, or other operations in, on, over or under land. The four-year period starts with the date on which the operations were "substantially completed".
- A change of use of any building, or any part of a building, to use as a single dwelling house.

The four-year period starts with the date of the breach. The unauthorised use will only be immune from planning enforcement action after four years if the unauthorised use was continuous. The four-year rule applies where the change of use to a single dwelling house involves:

- Development without planning permission; or
- Failure to comply with a condition or limitation attached to a planning permission.

The conversion of a building into separate self-contained flats is covered by the four-year rule. The conversion of live/work accommodation (sui-generis use) into a single dwelling house is also covered by the four-year rule.

Ten-year rule
No planning enforcement action can be taken after ten years, starting with the date of the breach, in respect of all other breaches of planning control including:
- Material change of use (other than a change of use to a single dwelling house, see four-year rule)
- Breach of condition (except a condition relating to use as a single dwelling house, see four-year rule)

The breach of an occupancy condition on a dwelling house, such as a condition requiring the property to be always occupied by an agricultural worker, is subject to the ten-year rule. The failure to comply with the occupancy condition does not result in a "change of use to use as a single dwelling house" as the property has always been a single dwelling house and therefore the four-year rule does not apply (see four-year rule).

The unauthorised use will only be immune from planning enforcement action after ten years if the unauthorised use was continuous. However it should be noted that where there has been deliberate concealment of a breach of planning control, local planning authorities may apply for a planning enforcement order to allow them to take action after the time limits set out above have expired.

Once planning permission has been granted,
You are at liberty to implement the consent immediately, however you are advised to wait, as planning permissions are subject to challenge and can be revoked.

Under section 77 of the TCPA 1990 the Secretary of State has powers to direct a local planning authority to refer an application to him for decision. This is known as a "called-in" application.

This power is not used very often, usually if the planning issues raised are of more than local importance. Where an application has been called-in usually an inquiry will be held. In England, the inquiry procedure is set out in the Town and Country Planning (Inquiries Procedure) (England) Rules 2000.

The High Court is the only authority that can formally identify a legal error in a planning inspector's or Secretary of State's decision and require that decision to be re-determined. Applications to challenge planning appeal decisions and decisions on called-in applications must be received by the Administrative Court within six weeks from the date of the decision.

So, where the decision is made by the Secretary of State (either appeal or called-in application) the time period for challenge is six weeks. Where a decision is made by a local planning authority, a challenge can also be made under a judicial review procedure, the period in which a review must be made is now also six weeks (reduced from three months.) There are no other third party right of appeals, apart from through the statutory review or judicial review process.

It is therefore advisable to wait at least six weeks and ensure that your planning permission is not being challenged before commencing works.

General: Planning Permission and Use Classes Related to Commercial Property

Commercial properties are covered by The Town and Country Planning (Uses Classes) Order 1987, which divides the uses of business properties and land into different categories. The lists below indicate the class types and how they can be utilised.

List of planning categories

A1: Shops	A2: Financial and Professional Services	A3: Restaurants and Cafes
A4: Drinking Establishments	A5: Hot Food Takeaways	
B1: Businesses	B2: General Industrial	B8: Storage and Distribution
C1: Hotels	C2: Residential Institutions	C2A: Secure Residential Institutions
C3: Dwelling Houses	C4: Houses in Multiple Occupation	
D1: Non-Residential Institutions	D2: Assembly and Leisure	Sui Generis
B3 – B7: Special Industrial Group A – E		

In some cases, the use of commercial property can be altered without reference to the local authority – i.e., from A5 takeaways to A1 shops. However, A3 restaurant to A5 takeaways use is not automatic. See below a list of changes of use that do not require planning permission. However, this is not definitive so when considering change of use you should seek advice from the local authority involved.

Changes that do not require planning permission

From	To
A2: Financial and Professional Services (When properties have a display window at ground level)	A1: Shops
A3: Restaurant and Cafes	A1: Shops A2: Financial and Professional Services
A4: Drinking Establishments	A1: Shops A2: Financial and Professional Services A3: Restaurants and Cafes
A5: Hot Takeaways	A1: Shops A2: Financial and Professional Services A3: Restaurants and Cafes

B1: Businesses (less than 235 sq m of floor space)	B8: Storage and Distribution
B2: General Industrial	B1: Businesses
B2: General Industrial (less than 235 sq m of floor space)	B8: Storage and Distribution
B8: Storage and Distribution (less than 235 sq m of floor space)	B1: Businesses
C4: Houses in Multiple Location	C3: Dwelling Houses
Casinos	D2: Assembly and Leisure

The table below indicates what types of use fall within each category.

A1: Shops	Shops, retail warehouses, hairdressers, undertakers, travel and ticket agencies, post office (not sorting offices), pet shops, sandwich bars, showrooms, domestic hire shops, dry cleaners, funeral directors and Internet cafes
A2: Financial and Professional Services	Financial Services such as banks and building societies, professional services (other than health)
A3: Restaurants and Cafes	For the sale of food and drink for consumption on the premises – restaurants, snack bars and cafes

Commercial Properties and the Planning System

A4: Drinking Establishments	Public houses, Wine bars or other drinking establishments (but not night clubs).
A5: Hot Food Takeaways	For the sale of hot food for consumption off the premises
B1: Businesses	Offices (other than those fall within A2 use), Research and development of products and processes, Light industry appropriate in a residential area
B2: General Industrial	Use for industrial process other than those fall within class B1 (excluding incineration purposes, chemical treatment or landfill or hazardous waste)
B8: Storage or Distribution	Including open air storage.
C1: Hotels	Hotels, boarding and guest houses where no significant element of care is provided (excludes hostels).
C2: Residential Institutions	Residential care homes, hospitals, nursing homes, boarding schools, residential colleges and training centres.
C2A: Secure Residential Institutions	Use for a provision of secure residential accommodation, including use as a prison, young offenders' institution, detention centre, secure training centre, custody centre, short term holding centre, secure hospital, secure local authority accommodation or use as a military barracks.
C3: Dwelling	This class is formed of 3 parts:

Houses	C3(a) covers use by a single person or a family (a couple whether married or not, a person related to one another with members of the family of one of the couple to be treated as members of the family of the other), an employer and certain domestic employees (such as an au pair, nanny, nurse, governess, servant, chauffeur, gardener, secretary and personal assistant), a carer and the person receiving the care and a foster parent and foster child. C3(b): up to six people living together as a single household and receiving care e.g. supported housing schemes such as those for people with learning disabilities or mental health problems. C3(c) allows for groups of people (up to six) living together as a single household. This allows for those groupings that do not fall within the C4 HMO definition, but which fell within the previous C3 use class, to be provided for i.e., a small religious community may fall into this section as could a homeowner who is living with a lodger.
C4: Houses in Multiple Occupation	Small, shared dwelling houses occupied by between three and six unrelated individuals, as their only or main residence, who share basic amenities such as a kitchen or bathroom.
D1: Non-Residential Institutions	Clinics, health centres, crèches, day nurseries, day centres, schools, art galleries (other than for sale or hire), museums, libraries, halls, places of worship, church halls, law court. Non residential education and training centres.

D2: Assembly and Leisure	Cinemas, music and concert halls, bingo and dance halls (but not night clubs), swimming baths, skating rinks, gymnasiums or area for indoor or outdoor sports and recreations (except for motor sports, or where firearms are used).
Sui Generis	Certain uses do not fall within any use class and are considered 'sui generis'. Such uses include: theatres, houses in multiple occupation, hostels providing no significant element of care, scrap yards. Petrol filling stations and shops selling and/or displaying motor vehicles. Retail warehouse clubs, nightclubs, launderettes, taxi businesses, amusement centres and casinos.

If the property is without planning permission for your intended use and the class cannot be altered, then a formal planning application will be required. This can be a lengthy process and will usually take at least eight weeks or more.

It is very useful to be armed with the above knowledge when you are planning to buy a commercial property for investment. In particular, it will come in useful if you plan to buy at auction, as many commercial properties sold at auction have exhausted their shelf-life, so to speak, and that is why they are being sold in that manner. However, if you are aware of the change of use possibilities then you can turn a redundant property into a sound investment.

The next chapter discusses the process of buying a commercial property at auction.

****

Chapter 7

Purchasing a Commercial Property at Auction

How Auctions Work

What is a property auction?
The process of sale in an auction is very similar to the normal method of private sale. However, for an auction sale the seller and their solicitor carry out all the necessary paperwork and legal investigations prior to the auction. Subject to the property receiving an acceptable bid, the property will be 'sold' on auction day with a legally binding exchange of contracts and a fixed completion date.

Different types of property auction houses
Auction houses vary in size and the amount of business that they conduct and the frequency with which they hold auctions. Most will

sell both residential and commercial property and each will have its own style of operation, and fee structure.

Large auction houses will hold auctions frequently, perhaps every two months and will have around 250 lots for sale. A lot of the auctions happen in London but will also be held nearer to home.

The medium size auction houses will hold auctions as frequently as they can, in regional venues, such as racecourses and conference centres, and depending on stock, usually every two to three months, tending to advertise locally. The small auction houses will have far fewer lots and will hold their sales in smaller local venues. They may advertise in local press but more often will trade on word of mouth.

Those who attend auctions

As you might imagine, all sorts of people attend auctions. The common denominator is that they are all interested in buying property.

Property investors are most common at auction, people who are starting out building a portfolio or those who have large portfolios that they wish to expand. They tend to fall into two groups, those who are after capital appreciation, i.e., buy at a low value and build the capital value and those who are looking for rental income. Then there are the property traders who like a quick profit from buying and 'flipping' property. These types usually have intimate knowledge of an area and are well placed to make a quick profit. Then we have the developers who look for small profitable sites or larger sites where property can be built and sold on. The sites can have existing buildings on them or can be vacant lots with or without planning permission. Last, but not least, we have those people who intend to buy solely for the purpose of owner occupation, look to buy a below- value property that they can redesign and make their own.

What types of property are suitable for auction?
There is strong demand for all types of properties offered at auction. These may be properties requiring updating, those with short leases, development sites with or without planning permission, repossessions, forced sales, investment properties, ground rents, probates, receivership sales and local authority properties. However, any type of property can be sold at auction and initially the property will be inspected to discuss specific criteria and the current situation. Extensive research will be carried out by the auction house and advice offered as to whether auction is the appropriate method of sale. The below represents a cross section of what might be found at auction.

Properties for Improvement
Properties in need of updating make ideal auction Lots. They are in great demand from refurbishment specialists and private buyers, keen to undertake a project for their own occupation or for resale. .

Development Propositions
Derelict or disused farm buildings, empty commercial premises, buildings with potential for conversion or change of use, can all sell well at auction. In some locations a change to residential can significantly add to the value of a property, in other situations there

may be space for additional dwellings or to substantially enlarge the property.

Building Land

There is no better way of ensuring a seller achieves best price for a building plot or parcel of development land than to offer it for sale by auction. Builders will be able to consult with architects, planners etc., and be ready to bid in the auction room.

Mixed Use Properties

Properties that have twin uses or a variety of potential future uses are ideal for sale by auction. Retail shops with accommodation above appeal to investors as well as owner-occupiers. Further conversion work can often be undertaken and the property tailored to suit the purchaser's special requirements.

Commercial Investments

Retail shops, offices, industrial units, garage blocks and parking areas - an ever increasing number of commercial investments are being sold at auction. It doesn't matter whether they are vacant or tenanted, with lease renewal soon needed or with a long way to run. As mentioned in the previous chapter, it is very useful to have some idea of the potential for change of use for such properties.

Unique Properties

There are always some rare entries, sought after property and prime locations that need to be sold in a competitive bidding environment. Unexpectedly high prices have been achieved by this route.

Amenity Land and Other Property
Paddocks, meadows, fields, moorings, amenity land and also other unusual land parcels are all sold at auction. If it is property or land that is surplus to requirements, the likelihood is a buyer can be found at auction. If it has a value, and is worth marketing, it is worth considering a disposal by auction.

The atmosphere of an auction room can be extremely exciting and competitive and it is often the case that an interested party will bid in excess of the figure that had previously been set as their maximum. In some cases, the prices achieved at auction can be higher than those achieved by private treaty.

How to Go About Finding a Property at Auction
There are many property auctions being held all over the UK every day. Where you choose to buy at auction very much depends on what you want to buy, what is the intended use for the property, residential investment, commercial investment, or a property for your own home.

Most people tend to concentrate on the area that they know. However, a few adventurous souls will branch out further afield. In order to find out the whereabouts of property auctions you will want to get hold of one of the main publications such as *Property Auction News* which is a magazine devoted entirely to property auctions in the UK. You will have to pay for this magazine by subscription, details of which can be found at www.propertyauctionnews.co.uk. The organ of the surveying world, The Estates Gazette, which is a weekly publication also features some property auctions.

One other invaluable source of information is the Essential Information Group. This is the news source for serious investors at auction. It is subscription based.

The Essential Information Group was formed in 1990 to provide the property industry with detailed information as to the results of all London property auctions. It now covers the whole of the UK and is recognised as the industry standard for auction information and currently includes details on over 500,000 properties and over 35,000 lots each year worth more than £5.5 billion. A range of services are available and they work closely with over 450 different auction houses arranging the transmission of guide prices, results and the provision of catalogues for interested parties. They also host a variety of Premium Rate services including a LiveLink service where people can listen live to an auction via telephone, thus allowing as many people as possible to access these auction details.
The EIG have close ties with many auction houses where they provide services for viewing live property auctions on the internet. You can check out their online auctions page to see what auctions are going to be broadcast live.

For more information on the Essential Information Group you should contact the address and website overleaf.

By Post	By Phone	By Email
Essential Information Group Charter House 9 Castlefield Road Reigate Surrey RH2 0SA	01737 226150 Fax: 01737 242 693	Account Enquiries: accounts@eigroup.co.uk Sales and subscription enquiries: sales@eigroup.co.uk www.eiggroup.co.uk

Once you have found the auction houses(s) that you want to deal with you can go on their mailing list. There are a number of websites that provide free auction lists, such as www.propertyauctionaction.co.uk. You can also often find auction catalogues online at the auction house website.

Perusing the auctioneer's catalogue

An auction house will release their catalogue several weeks before the auction begins. The catalogue will be in hard copy form or electronic form. This doesn't give much time for the prospective purchaser to look at what is on offer and arrange a viewing and get everything else in order. However, that is the nature of auctions. Quick processes and quick disposals.

The catalogue starts with the lot number and then a photo, usually one photo but sometimes more. the viewing dates are listed along with the address and the status, i.e., available, along with the category, in this case vacant commercial. The venue of the auction is mentioned and the date, along with who instructed the property to auction.

Then the catalogue will provide property details and location followed by more detail as to the property size and numbers of rooms, parking etc. The information in the catalogue should provide sufficient detail to enable the prospective purchaser to go to the next stage and view the property then attend the auction.

The order of lots in the catalogue

An auction catalogue consists of Lots, and they will be numbered in the order at which they will be sold at auction. It is the practice of some auction houses to put the most popular lot at the start of the auction so as to draw bidders in. They will also intersperse less popular lots with the popular lots to ensure that bidder levels are maintained and people don't drift away after the 'sexy' lots have sold. It is important to remember that auction houses want to create an atmosphere of excitement on the day so that people will bid for what is on offer.

The guide price

The guide prices for properties at auction will vary, depending on what is for sale and where it is. Market forces will dictate this, as they do for property sold in the conventional way. However, for a good many properties the price will be set low, which reflects the condition of the property and also reflects the fact that the auctioneer wants to draw people in to bidding. In many cases, auctioneers will drop the guide price at the outset as most people won't start bidding at the actual starting price. Therefore, you will find that if a house/commercial property is valued at £60,000 the auctioneer will open with this then drop down to £50,000 to start the bidding.

Guide prices are dictated by the reserve price on the lot. Sellers will have a price that they will not go under. This price is not disclosed to potential bidders before the auction but will affect the price at which the auctioneer starts the process. So, if a property is £60,000 and the auctioneer starts at £50,000 then £50,000 will be at the reserve price or just above.

Finding a property suitable for you in an auction catalogue

Once you have either been sent, or downloaded, a catalogue then you will need to identify the property or properties that you want to view and are interested in bidding for. There is quite a lot of background work to do before the auction begins. You will usually have about two weeks to start the ball rolling. After having identified a property suitable for you, you will need to arrange a viewing.

Viewing an auction property

As we have seen above with the auctioneers' particulars, viewing times are usually set by the auction and shown in their catalogue and you will have to fit in with these times. They are very much like estate agents block bookings. The number of viewings is limited and you will usually get the opportunity to view three or four times before auction. The people who show the property will not usually have any idea about the details of the property, being employed as key holders to show interested parties around. They will take details of all those who have viewed. The viewings are in half-hour slots.

Although the viewing times are stated in the catalogue it is always best to play safe and confirm the times as they can change. If you have travelled a long way to attend a viewing only to find out it has been cancelled or rescheduled this can be very annoying, to say the least. You will need to get used to the fact that if a property is popular and attracting lots of interest then there may be lots of people waiting at the property on the allotted day and time. However, you are there for a reason and need to keep your wits about you and take all the necessary notes. You will be greatly aided by doing adequate research, even before you get round to viewing the property. When you go to a viewing make sure you have the following:

- A tape measure. Check the measurements against those stated in the auction catalogue. You can also use this date for your own plans.
- Camera. This probably goes without saying but you need to get accurate photos of the building, exterior and interior, to act as a record and help you with your own plans.
- A torch. The property may be dark inside and you need to know what you are looking at. Also, a torch may be needed for safety reasons, depending on the condition of the property.
- A note pad or means of taking notes. This is very important as you may need to take copious notes to aid you in making your decision.
- If you can, take a small portable ladder. This should enable you to look into areas such as loft spaces or cupboards etc.

Using a surveyor

If you are not experienced in carrying out basic property surveys then you might want to employ the services of a surveyor. This might cost, but you will get a firm idea of the structural condition of the property in question. You might want to do several viewings of the property, the first one yourself and then, if needs be, with a surveyor.

The notepad and camera will come in very useful the first time around. You should ensure that you take photos of the external and internal areas of the property. The following are areas that you will want to inspect, and which a surveyor would inspect:

- The envelope of the building. This includes the roof. You should check the roof timbers, tiles, condition of the covering such as the asphalt or felt and if it is a flat roof check for signs of standing water as this indicates that there are problems with the drainage. You might want to look at the eaves of the building, particularly if you wish to convert a loft or install a mansard (roof extension)
- Electrics and plumbing. With the plumbing you need to locate stopcocks and ascertain the condition of the boiler. Check the external guttering and the condition of the soil stack. With the electrics check the age and state of the fuse board which will give you some idea of the state of the wiring. Check wall sockets and check to see if you can see any wiring to ascertain the condition. Look into the loft to see if there are any wires running around. Whilst in the loft look at the existing loft insulation and look up to see if you can see any daylight, which will indicate roof problems.

- Damp. Check for signs of damp-take photographs so you can ascertain whether it is rising or penetrating damp and just what the extent of work might be.
- Structure of the building. Look closely at the condition of the walls externally or whether there are any signs of movement or cracking and look for evidence of movement around door frames and windows and also floor levels.
- Gardens/outside spaces. These areas are quite often ignored by potential bidders. You should look at the condition of gardens, fences and also note any boundary lines. To refurbish an outside area takes a lot of time and money and you will want to get this right.

Types of Surveys

The following gives a very brief overview of the different surveys available. These are of use when purchasing a commercial property. There are other types for residential property. When considering the possible purchase of the property the choices are as follows:
- Full Building Survey (most popular survey for most properties).
- Valuation only.
- Structural Inspection (General and Specific).
- Home Condition Survey and RICS Condition Survey

The Day of the Auction

Having armed yourself with all you need to know about a particular property, it is assumed that you are comfortable with the property you have selected to purchase at auction and the auction day has arrived. Before you set off to the auction, phone the auction house to make sure the auction is still taking place at the published venue and time and that the lot you are interested in has not been withdrawn.

If you are successful in bidding for your lot then you will need to put down a deposit of ten percent. Sometimes if the value of the property is less than twenty thousand pounds then the minimum deposit is two thousand pounds. The deposit cannot be paid for in cash or credit card and you must take along two items for proof of identity such as a passport and utility bill.

Make sure you arrive at the auction at least an hour before the auction starts. This will give you time to register, if necessary, and to check any last-minute special conditions relating to your lot. Some auction houses require you to register, then give you a card with a number on it so that if you are the successful bidder for a lot then you are easily identifiable. Familiarise yourself with the auction room and find a place where you have good vision of all the other bidders so you can get an idea of who is bidding against you.

The role of the auctioneer
In the auction room, the main person is the auctioneer. It is his or her skill in selling the property that dominates. It is the job of the auctioneer to get the highest price that they can for the property, both for the vendor and for their own fee income.

Auctioneers will have different styles of conducting sales depending on where the auction house is and the culture of a particular house. Their styles will range from the cajoling to try to get more bids, to the aggressive to try to at least rise above the reserve price.

Notwithstanding their own individual styles, they are all bound by a common code of conduct. The auctioneer will reserve the right to bid on behalf of the vendor. The auctioneer will state this in his or her opening words. What this really means in practice is that, if the bidding has not reached the reserve price, then the auctioneer can take a bid 'off the wall' to try to up the bids to the reserve price. This is known as 'chandelier bidding'.

Bidding for your lot
You will want to be in a position where you can be clearly seen by the auctioneer. If you have a lot in your sights then you will want to ensure that, when the time comes for a bid, you can be clearly seen and heard. The best tactic is to arrive as early as possible and to obtain a prominent seat, as close to the front as possible but not right at the front.

When the auction starts the auctioneer will direct you to a copy of the general conditions of sale for the auction but will not actually read them out. You should be familiar with them before the auction. They will briefly explain the bidding process and then the auction will begin. The auctioneer will give a very brief description of the lot and then ask for the bidding to begin. As a rough estimate the auctioneer will process between twenty and twenty-five lots per hour though this may vary.

When the auctioneer announces your lot, it is time for you to go into action. Make sure you bid clearly so that the auctioneer registers your bid. The old myth that if you scratch your nose you have made a bid is not true. Your bid will only be registered if the auctioneer sees a definite gesture. The bidding process is quite organised with the auctioneer only ever registering the bids of two people until one drops out and then they look for another bidder. You may not even get to bid if the current bidders go above your ceiling. Telephone bids are quite common with someone from the auction house bidding on behalf of the person on the telephone. Quite often the auctioneer will open the bidding with one person making a bid and then no other bids until the auctioneer has announced the property will be sold on the third and final asking.

At this point just as the hammer is about to come down someone makes a bid and the bidding war starts. Keep in mind the ceiling price that you calculated before the auction and stop bidding when the price gets to your limit. Do not get carried away with the emotion of the auction room and start bidding above the limit you set yourself before the auction. If you are successful in your bid for your desired lot then you may be asked to hold up the card with the number given to you when you registered for the auction and a member of the auction house staff will come to find you.

Bidding in increments
What to bid is quite important. If you think that the property is yours if you bid way above the reserve price too soon then you might find that you have paid too much. Better bidding in increments to keep the rises in check. You can bid late by jumping in at the last moment, taking everyone by surprise and knocking them off balance. In this way you can achieve what you want.

If you are successful in your bid, there will be some forms to fill in and the deposit to be paid plus a fee to the auction house that is usually up to £750 although this will vary and can be lower or higher. You should ensure that you have the following on you when you go to auction:

- Photographic proof of identification. This can be a passport or driving licence
- Proof of residential address with a bill or bank statement dated within the last three months
- Cleared funds, i.e., proof that you can pay your 10% deposit then and there.

The balance of the money will be required to be paid by you within twenty-eight days although sometimes you may have to complete within fourteen days if stipulated by the vendor. Make sure your solicitor is aware that time is of the essence and that you need to complete quickly.

Unsold property at auction

Around three quarters of all property at auction is usually sold. This will depend on the auction and what is for sale. However, If the bids for a property are not accepted because they do not reach a level close enough to the reserve price that has been set for the property then the lot will be withdrawn from the auction (sometimes left to the auctioneer's discretion at the instruction of the seller). If you are still interested in the property then see the auctioneer after the auction. There may be a deal to be done with the vendor. Many buyers will do a deal with the seller after the auction if the property remains unsold. This is known as 'Hawking'.

If you buy after auction then auction conditions still apply and time is of the essence. If others are interested in the same property, it is the first person to submit money and exchange contracts who will win.

Withdrawn property

Sometimes and for no apparent reason the property that you are interested in might be withdrawn. This could be that the vendor has sold pre-auction or that there are problems with the estate. If you have spent any money prior to auction on checking the property out, either surveyors' costs or legal costs, then you will lose this as the vendor has no responsibility for any losses incurred.

****

FOR THE SMALLER INVESTOR: MANAGING YOUR COMMERCIAL PROPERTY PORTFOLIO-GENERAL ADVICE

Chapter 8

Business Leases Generally

In the previous chapters, we have seen how you can get involved in the commercial property sector, from entry through special funds and through acquiring your own property at an auction. We have also discussed funding generally, through banks and through a Self-Invested Personal Pension Scheme.

In Chapters 8-13 we concentrate specifically on aspects of managing commercial property, which will be of use to the smaller investor who has bought a property for investment, smaller lots, and wishes to either manage the property alone or wants to know more about all aspects of management, from entering into a lease, service charges, repairing responsibilities, insurance and the law generally when it comes to rent reviews and renewing leases. We begin with business leases generally.

This chapter deals generally with business leases and sets out the basic framework that governs these sorts of agreements. The fundamental principles of business leases are dealt with in the next chapter.

Many people entering into a business lease do not have a clear idea of what it is they are entering into. This is most often the case with those involved in setting up a business for the first time. The agreement signed between landlord and tenant is often the single most expensive business item and it is potentially the area that will result in future problems if a clear understanding is not gained at the outset. Those new to business leases will find themselves confronted with a series of technical terms, some of which are interchangeable and are used throughout this book.

These terms are as follows:

Lease or demise
A lease is a formal document under which land and premises is "demised" or leased to a tenant. Demised premises is a label for the land with a building or buildings.

Landlord or lessor
These alternative terms are used to describe the estate owner who grants the lease in question. A landlord can be a freeholder (outright owner) or head leaseholder.

Tenant or lessee
These interchangeable words describe a person who accepts a lease.

Assignor or Assignee
By assignment is meant the outright transfer of the lease to another person. The assignor is the person transferring and the assignee the person accepting.

Sub leases (sub demises)

A Sub-lease takes place when a person already has a lease from a head landlord and that person creates another lease to someone else.

The relationship of the landlord to the leaseholder (tenant)

The relationship of the landlord to the tenant arises where one person who owns either the freehold or a leasehold interest in a property grants to another an interest which is lesser than his own term. The creation of a lease, correctly executed, passes a legal estate in land to the tenant. The lease must either be for a "term certain" or fixed term i.e., 5, 10 or 20 years, or for a periodic term, which runs from week to week or month to month and is capable of being ended by notice to quit from either party. On the termination of a fixed term lease or periodic tenancy, at the end of the term, the tenant's estate in land ends. However, the rules governing the ending of business leases are laid out clearly in the Landlord and Tenant Act 1954, Part 2, and unless a strict notice procedure prescribed by the Act is followed, then the lease will continue as a statutory tenancy. As we will see in Chapter 13, a business tenant has very clear rights to the continuation of a tenancy and the grant of a new tenancy unless the landlord has strong reasons for preventing this.

A lease, because it creates an estate in land, is much more than a mere personal or contractual agreement for the occupation of land by a tenant. *A lease confers a right in property, enabling the tenant to exclude all third parties including the landlord from* possession for the duration of the lease, in return for the payment of rent.

A lease is distinct from a mere license to occupy, which confers no exclusive possession but merely gives the right to use a premises for strictly limited purposes.

If a written agreement for the occupation of any land or premises, whether residential or business contains three elements then it will be a lease or tenancy. These are:

-the grant of exclusive possession
-at a rent or for periodical payments
-for a fixed or periodic term.

It is not the intention to discuss further the distinction between license and tenancy. This book is intended for those who have signed a business tenancy/long lease and the above is for general guidance only.

The creation and the form of a business lease
A business lease is a conveyance in land and is as initially complex and time consuming (and expensive) as buying and selling any property. What seems simple on the face of it, especially for the frustrated would-be businessperson, who expects to come into possession of his or her property relatively quickly, is in reality a complicated process which must be approached cautiously. For the person entering into a business lease, there are three distinct stages in the overall transaction that it is important to be aware of:

-preliminary negotiations
-a contract or agreement for a lease
-the lease itself

Preliminary negotiations

This is the stage when the initial bargaining goes on, the property is inspected, the rent and other terms are discussed and references given on the part of the tenant. At this stage, either party remains free to withdraw under law. A contract is only concluded when the parties reach agreement on the granting of a lease. The role of agents in the process of negotiation will be discussed a little later in chapter two.

Contract for a lease

A contract for the leasing of land is not enforceable unless it is in writing. The prospective landlord promises that he will grant the lease and the prospective tenant promises that he will take the lease on the terms agreed. Finally, the lease is granted from this initial agreement and an estate in land is granted. One general rule is that for an estate in land to be created it must be effected by deed. This deed will be incorporated within the document created as the lease and will contain the words "deed of grant". Another general, but important, rule, is that a lease must be in writing and witnessed to be enforceable in court. Again, the law surrounding this is complex and is beyond the scope of this book, suffice to say that the general principles mentioned above form the main body of the law.

The main terms of a lease

A business lease, in common with all leases, will contain the following main terms:

- The names of the parties, or their agents, or other sufficient description which will identify them. A general description will not usually suffice.
- The address of the property or a sufficient enough description to identify it.
- The term of the lease and the commencement date
- The rent and any premium for the premises. Quite often, in addition to rent, a premium, or one-off payment, usually for "goodwill" will have to be paid.
- Landlord's covenants and tenants covenants. The meaning of covenants, which are basically undertakings, is discussed in greater detail below.

Most leases will contain standard clauses relating to repairing obligations, payment of rent, subletting and other general terms such as behaviour of tenant, overall use of the premises, assignment (transfer of lease) etc.

A lease and counterpart (duplicate) is usually prepared by the landlord's solicitor who will send the draft form of lease to the tenant's solicitor. The normal practice is for the tenant to bear all reasonable costs of the transaction. It is very important, if you are entering into a lease, to obtain quotes for the work beforehand and to get a clear idea of the overall costs, including disbursements, such as stamp duty and land registration fees. All conveyances of land have to be registered with the land registry. Business leases will attract stamp duty, the amount of which can be checked with a solicitor and which was detailed in chapter 3?

Rights and obligations of parties under a lease

The rights and obligations of parties to any lease are governed by the *covenants* in the lease. There are three basic types of covenant:

Express covenants, which regulate the exact nature and scope of each party's rights and obligations. These are discussed in greater depth further on.

Implied covenants. These apply only so far as a lease fails to expressly provide for a matter but the implication on entering the contract is that a right or obligation exists.

Statutorily implied covenants which usually override the terms of the lease, the main principle being that statute overrides contract. Laws passed by Parliament and entered onto the statute form the basis of statutorily implied covenants.

All express covenants should be read clearly as these will form the framework for the relationship between landlord and tenant and, once entered into cannot be varied without either the agreement of the landlord or an order of court.

Examples of express covenants are those of rent, repairing obligations, insurance liabilities, use of premises, subletting and assignment. At common law, a tenant has the freedom to assign and any covenants to the contrary must be expressly imposed. As we will see a little later, a landlords consent to assignment cannot be unreasonably withheld. With business leases, the consent to assign is usually hedged with specific requirements relating to the premises in question, i.e., that the user will continue to use the premises for the use for which they are intended.

The lease will usually contain detailed provisions relating to service charges and these are discussed in more depth in chapter 6. It is also important that the consequences of non-payment of rent are understood. Usually, non-payment of rent on a given date will result in the charging of interest on monies not paid. Depending on the managing agent this either will or will not be levied. It is important to alert the owner or agent to the possibility of late or delayed payments in order to avoid bad feeling and possible legal action.

Rent reviews

A new rent for a property is more likely to be the letting value of a property in the open market at the time of rent review. The exercise involves looking at comparables in the area and drawing comparisons before arriving at a rental figure.

While it is usual for a rent to be agreed, assuming that an open market rent is easily calculated, it is absolutely essential that a clause be inserted in the lease which tells either party how the rent will be arrived at in the event of disagreement. Solicitors or property advisors should be able to advise on the nature and extent of arbitration should an agreement not be reached. Sometimes, an independent expert will be provided for, otherwise alternative dispute resolution should be considered. This will be discussed in more detail further on. The following are examples of the ways that rent can be revised:

Upwards only. This means that the rent will either be increased or will stay the same. It cannot be reduced. This is called an "Upwards Only" clause.

Minimum base rent. The rent cannot fall below the rent first payable at the beginning of the lease but subject to that can go up or down depending on the market value at the time of the review.

Open Market Value. The rent will simply be subject to market forces at the time of review and can therefore go up or down.

Turnover rent. A turnover rent is normally either a combination of a base rent and an element reflecting a tenant's turnover, or a simple percentage of turnover.

Index linked. This means that the rent review, and subsequent increase will be linked to a given index, such as the Retail Price Index.

Fixed increases. In this case the lease will simply state when and by how much the rent will be increased.

It is very important that the prospective tenant is clear about rent and rent reviews before taking on a lease. Property advisors will usually give a considered opinion. However, questions such as "how much will the rent be in five years time" are impossible to answer as, unless there is a specific clause in a lease concerning rental increase then market forces will always prevail.

Maintenance obligations

The obligation to carry out repairs under a lease will vary. However, there is a main principle and that is that, notwithstanding whose responsibility it is to actually carry out the repairs, the tenant will always pay. This will either be by way of a direct payment or through service charges.

Directly related to the above principle, some leases are referred to as *full repairing and insurance leases*. In addition to repairs, the tenant is liable for insurance costs. Where there are several tenants, each will normally be responsible for the internal repair of their part of the premises and for contributing towards the landlord's costs of maintaining the exterior, structure and common parts.

Given that repairs and maintenance to a property will vary according to the state of the property and the attitude of the landlord, it is very advisable for a prospective tenant to instruct a chartered surveyor to undertake a survey of the premises.

This will help with negotiating and assessing the implications of the repairing obligations, which are to apply at the beginning, during and at the end of the lease. (See appendix 2 – sample business lease).

The lease, or a supplementary agreement may include a record of the survey, together with photographic evidence of condition (called a schedule of condition) which may, with the agreement of individuals provide a benchmark for future repair work. This will also enable the tenant to work out likely outgoings over the course of the lease.

The ability of the tenant to carry out a survey will generally be dictated by the size of the building. In larger buildings it is impractical to carry out a survey and the overall maintenance will be, or should be, managed through a service charge. It is essential for a prospective tenant to understand the framework governing the collection and use of service charges. This is discussed further in chapter 6.

Towards the end of the lease term, notwithstanding the tenant's attitude towards renewal the landlord will normally serve a notice on the tenant requiring the tenant to carry out certain repairs to bring the building back up to the standard of the original at the time of taking on the lease. This is called a "schedule of dilapidation's". It is very common for there to be disagreement over these, particularly where the management during the lease term has been lax and virtually no repairs have been carried out. The effect of this is that repairs have been stored up and there will be heavy expenditure at the end.

Landlords vary, and their skill, ability and attitudes will also vary. So will the attitudes of any managing agents employed. It is very important and advisable to obtain professional opinion if faced with a schedule of dilapidation's that you disagree with. The costs of employing a professional advisor may be more than offset by the savings achieved on any repairs demanded.

The ultimate goal of landlord and tenant is to manage in an efficient manner during the course of the lease and to ensure that expenditure on repairs and maintenance is even throughout the lease term. The worse scenario and the most problematic is trying to put a badly maintained building back to rights.

Insurance

The terms of a business lease will vary in relation to the provision of insurance. However, in much the same way as repairing obligations, there is one main principle. Regardless of who arranges the insurance, the tenant will pay the premiums.

The main form of insurance for a premises is usually buildings insurance, which will pay for any identified insurable risks, ranging from fire to flood damage, from partial damage to outright destruction. Many policies will not cater for "Acts of God" such as earthquake. However, there are relatively few earthquakes in Britain so this is not a real problem. In addition to buildings insurance, there will always be a requirement for public liability insurance, which will usually be arranged by the tenant.

In addition to these two main forms of insurance a tenant may be required under a lease to provide insurance for plate glass, if relevant in the event of window breakage. Even if this is not required the tenant should consider getting adequate cover as the cost of replacing broken windows can be prohibitive. The premium will vary depending on the location of the shop. If the premises are situated next to a notorious pub, then it is likely that an insurer will charge more than if the shop was tucked away in a little side street.

In relation to buildings insurance, if the tenancy is of new-build premises, the role of insurance is crucial, as a distinction needs to be made between the insurer's liabilities and developer's liabilities. Normally, the managing agents or the owner would be taking charge of this area.

Sometimes the lease will give the landlord or the tenant the right to end the lease if the premises are very badly damaged, rather than reinstate them. Where the damage is insured there may be important questions about how, why and by whom the insurance money is spent and the parties will need to take professional advice at the outset.

Tenants should consider taking out their own insurance in respect of loss or damage of contents. Obviously, if a lot of time and money has been spent fitting out a shop and there is a break-in then the presence of a comprehensive insurance policy will go a long way to rectifying the situation and to enable the tenant to begin trading as soon as possible. Insurance can also be taken out to cover loss of profits. Tenants should check that the provisions for suspension of rent following insured damage are either indefinite or sufficiently long to enable the reinstatement of the building to take place.

It is a fact that, as with household insurance, many of those involved in business will not take out adequate insurance cover in order to save on money and reduce outgoings. However, as we have discussed, certain insurances are a requirement of the lease, such as buildings insurance and public liability insurance. Other insurance, such as contents, loss of profits and damage to plate glass are essential and should not be ignored. At the outset they should be factored in as a cost. It is also essential that a business tenant has a copy of the insurance policy in force and understands the full extent of cover. There are quite often incidences where the tenant will pay out unnecessarily for works which are insurable.

Use of premises subject to the lease
The lease will define the use to which premises can be put. However, this will also be determined by planning regulations

affecting the building and an area. For example, a parade of shops will have a predetermined use and this will be rigidly defined. The relevant planning class is usually outlined in a lease.

Some business premises contain a mixture of commercial and residential (the flat above the shop). A lease will also contain strict provisions regulating the use of the residential area, usually stipulating no subletting of part and intending the user of the business premises to occupy the residence as a home. If you intend to let such a premises then it is very important that you are clear about the uses to which the whole premises can be put. Appendix 2 shows an example lease for a typical mixed commercial/residential premises.

****

Chapter 9

Service Charges and Business Leases

Although there is comprehensive provision for residential properties, principally flats, for service charges, under the Landlord and Tenant Acts 1985/1987 and 1996, plus the Commonhold and Leasehold Reform Act 2002, the Acts do not apply to business premises.

The framework that applies to residential properties, however, forms the basis of good practice for the delivery of services, the charging and the accounting for services to business premises.

Service charges, normally levied when 2 or more business units are joined, are those charges over and above the rent charged for a property. Rent usually provides a profit to the owner and will not cover any additional costs associated with the upkeep of the property, such as the reasonable costs of repair, maintenance and replacement of the fabric, plant and equipment and materials necessary for the property. In addition, there will be common parts, which will need to be heated and adequately lit and gardens and other amenity areas, which need to be serviced.

Another charge, which may be included in a service charge, will be that of longer-term major repairs or replacements. This will have to be justified by the landlord as not many business tenants like their money being tied up in this way.

Sometimes, staff will need to be employed, particularly if the unit is part of a larger retailing centre and these costs will be passed on, along with any ongoing contracts to maintain and repair plant and equipment, such as lifts and escalators.

The landlord may wish to charge insurance through the service charge and will also usually charge an administration fee to cover the costs of staff time in managing services. This will normally be about 10% of the overall costs of services. Service charge costs should not otherwise include:

-any initial capital costs incurred in relation to the original design and construction of the fabric of the building, plant, or equipment
-any setting up costs which are reasonably to be considered as part of the original development cost of the property.

Capital improvement costs above the costs of normal maintenance, repair or replacement.

Future redevelopment costs
such costs as are matters between the owner and an individual occupier via enforcements of covenants for collection of rent, costs of letting units, consents for assignments, sub-letting, alterations, rent reviews etc.

Ultimately, one of the fundamental principles underpinning provision for services is that the services should be relevant and beneficial to the needs of the property, the owner, the tenant and the customers. Excessive profits should not be made and all costs should be accounted for. A budget should be produced for consultation about three months prior to the start of the financial year.

Value for money
Disputes about service charges, whether residential or business property, are frequent, long, drawn out and expensive and the management of charges is always under scrutiny. Therefore, it is essential that value for money is achieved.

Service quality should be appropriate to the location, age, use and character of the property. The owner should seek to achieve that service quality as cost effectively as possible, costs should be kept under review and, where appropriate, contractors and suppliers should be regularly required to submit competitive tenders or to provide competing quotations. Contractors and suppliers of services should be required to perform to written performance standards agreed with the owners and tenants.

Service charge apportionments
Another fundamental principle of service charge management is that of fair apportionment. This is undoubtedly one of the most difficult areas to get right. Leases will normally spell out the basis for apportionment, and the formula will be arrived at depending on the number of properties, their position in relation to the consumption of individual services and the nature of the overall property.

Service charges will usually be apportioned through the use of percentages or by a straight division, whichever is the more equitable. For example, if a shopping centre is on three floors, is it fair that the ground floor pays for lift depreciation, annual maintenance contracts and wear and tear of escalators? The answer would probably be yes because shoppers take advantage of the whole site and all ultimately benefit. It is usually easier to divide by the straight-line method in which all pay equally.

Taking on board the above, the following key principles of apportionment should apply:

- Apportionment of costs to each occupier should be on a fair and reasonable basis, in accordance with the principles of good estate management and applied fairly and consistently throughout the property having regard to the physical size, nature of use and the benefit to the occupier or occupiers.
- The occupiers should not be charged through the service charge or otherwise collectively towards costs attributable to un-let premises. Also, the cost of a special concession by an owner to any one occupier should be met by the owner.
- The owner should bear a fair proportion of the costs attributable to his use of the property, e.g. where a centre management suite is used in part as an owners regional office.
- If the property is fully let the owner should normally be able to recover all expenditure on services through the service charges.
- The estimated budget of service charge expenditure and certificated accounts should set out the method used to determine each occupiers share of the costs.

The above are a few of the key considerations when looking at apportionment of charges to business tenants.

Consultation with business users

The Landlord and Tenant Act 1985 (as amended) sets out a rigorous framework for consultation for residential occupiers of flats. This lays down a framework within which landlords must consult when expenditure is over a certain limit and also prescribes a time period and the need to supply estimates and allow feedback.

There is no such legislative requirement for business premises. However, the principles underlying the 1985 Act (as amended) inform the spirit of good practice underlying service charge provision to commercial premises.

Effective managers will always realize that communication between managers and tenants is essential to arrive at consensus. If large amounts of money are to be spent or there is to be a change in services and the cost of services then adequate notice should be given to tenants to allow them to voice opinion. If the work is costly then several estimates should be obtained and these sent to tenants and their opinion sought.

Although there is no formal legal framework governing the provision of services to commercial property there is always the **lease** *which will serve as the main document in any dispute. Ultimately, the tenant can always sue in the county court, alleging breach of contract or general inequity.*

Estimated budget expenditure

As with all service charges, whether residential or business, an estimate of expenditure for the forthcoming year has to be produced, in order to give tenants the opportunity to feed back and, if necessary, object to the forthcoming charges.

The budget will always coincide with the financial year of the organization or individual in question. If significant charges are made then this will be stipulated in the lease. If, for example, the financial year begins on the 1$^{st\ of}$ April each year, ending on the 31st March the next year then the budget for the forthcoming year should be presented at the latest by the beginning of February, to business tenants.

The budget should be broken down into individual heads of charge and be in a consistent format from year to year. The individual occupiers share of expenditure should be clearly set out in the budget. Explanation should be provided if there is a significant variation of costs over the previous year and also the previous years accounts should be laid out alongside the anticipated expenditure in order for the tenant to be able to interpret information.

Normally, and depending of course on the size of a scheme, a meeting will be held several months before the start of the financial year in order to discuss charges and answer any questions. This is seen as good practice and essential if good relations are to be maintained with tenants. If a letter and the figures are sent out to tenants without a prior meeting, it is likely that a lot of time will be spent dealing with queries.

The provision of certified accounts
The lease will normally outline the framework for the preparation of certified accounts and the provision of such to tenants. The Landlord and Tenant Acts 1985/1987 (as amended) lay down the requirements for residential leaseholders. The spirit of the Act flows

through the principles and practice of commercial property management. The following summarises good practice:

The owner should normally submit certified accounts to the occupiers in a timely manner and, in any event, within six months of the year-end (end of service charge year).

The accounts should give a reasonably comprehensive level of detail to enable occupiers to compare expenditure against estimated budget. Given the difference between the outlook of the financial professions and the average person, it is also very wise indeed to send out a management letter to tenants, which elaborates on each head of expenditure and explains any marked differences.

The owner should allow occupiers a reasonable time to feed back on the accounts and to raise queries.

Owners should deal with reasonable enquiries in a prompt and efficient manner and make relevant documentation available for inspection. It is usual for tenants to wish to see invoices for the year in question. Where copies are made available, a reasonable fee may be charged.

An auditor should certify the accounts, with the costs charged to the service charge accounts. If an occupier requests his own audit, the owner should agree and the audit fee charged to the occupier.

It is good practice, as with budgets, to hold a meeting to discuss audited accounts. A single letter to business users, even with a management letter can result in so much confusion that solicitors can be employed to deal with the query, which again results in valuable time being eaten up and ill feeling created. Nothing can replace initial face-to-face communication, followed by prompt action regarding queries.

Sinking funds

As mentioned previously, sometimes it is prudent, and necessary, to charge a sinking fund, which is designed to cater for longer-term maintenance and replacement of items. This will build up in an interest-bearing account. The fund should be built up on the basis of a plan, usually based on a survey of the building and associated components, such as lift replacements. The Landlord and Tenant Acts 1985/1987 (as amended) regulate the use of monies placed in a sinking fund for residential properties. This act requires that money be placed on trust for the tenants so that it is not affected by any actions against the owner, such as liquidation. In addition, there are clear requirements that it should be accounted for.

The same principles will apply to commercial properties. Good practice dictates that and money raised for longer term repairs, such as cyclical redecoration and repairs, and also replacements of capital items and major repairs to the building, along with any funds designed to replace furnishings and floor coverings, should be separated out into interest bearing client accounts, or trust accounts, separate from the owners' own monies.

The management of service charges is an extremely important area and is also an area prone to litigation. It is also usually an area, particularly in larger retail centres, that is normally undertaken by professionals. In smaller premises, it will normally be undertaken by a managing agent or an owner, but the same rigorous principles should apply.

Chapter 10

Assignment and Subletting of Business Leases

One of the main principles underlying the purchase of a leasehold interest in land is that the leaseholder has the right, generally subject to the permission of the landlord, which cannot unreasonably be withheld, to assign (pass on, through sale usually or can be paying someone to take on the lease) or sublet the premises (whole not part).

The subletting of a premises means the granting of a sublease, under the same terms and conditions, to someone else.

There will normally be a restriction, to some extent, on the lessee's right to assign or sublet or share the premises. The assignment of only part of the premises is usually prohibited.

Often the lease provides that the tenant must obtain the landlords consent to assign or sublet. The consent will usually depend on the potential assignee passing some form of test by meeting certain criteria. In some cases, the test takes the form of the landlord exercising some form of subjective judgment and in most of these cases the landlord's consent cannot be unreasonably withheld and the landlord cannot demand money as a condition of getting it.

In other cases, the landlord will have set objective tests which simply have to be met, the landlord exercising no discretion.

The legal framework regulating the landlords and tenants' actions is the 1988 Landlord and Tenant Act, which imposes the following duties on the landlord:

"Where the tenant serves on the landlord or other person who may consent, a notice to assign, the landlord owes the tenant a duty, within a reasonable time:

-to give consent, except where it is not reasonable to do so.

-to serve on the tenant written notice of his decision, whether or not he gives consent".

Where a notice is served, it must specify any conditions attached to consent, or the reasons for withholding it, as the case may be. The 1988 Act cannot be evaded by imposing an unreasonable condition to avoid giving consent.

If a landlord receives a written consent application, where, in addition to his own consent, the consent of a superior landlord is required as well, then the recipient is bound to take reasonable steps to secure the receipt within a reasonable time of a copy of the application by that person.

A landlord or superior landlord who is under the above duties must show, if challenged by the tenant, that he gave consent within a reasonable time. Likewise, the onus is on a landlord or superior landlord to show that any condition is reasonable, where the 1988 Act applies, and if consent is refused then the onus is on the landlord to show that refusal was reasonable.

The following general principles govern the question of whether refusal was reasonable:

- A landlord is not entitled to refuse consent to an assignment on grounds which have nothing to do with the relationship of landlord and tenant regarding the subject matter of the particular demise of the premises, such as an alleged difficulty in re-letting other premises.
- If the landlord refuses consent to a proposed assignment or sub-letting because of general reasons of good estate management relating to the whole building, not the particular part let to the tenant, the refusal will be unreasonable.
- It is not necessary for the landlord to prove that the conclusions which led him to refuse consent were justified, if they were conclusions reasonably reached in the circumstances.
- It may be reasonable for a landlord to refuse consent to a proposed assignment on the ground of the purpose for which the assignee wishes to use the premises, even though that purpose is not forbidden by the terms of the lease.

Examples of reasonable withholding of consent

A landlords reasonable withholding of consent has been held to be reasonable where the landlord believed that the proposed assignee or sub tenant was objectionable for some personal or financial reasons, or that the future earnings or financial viability of the property would be endangered. In addition, a landlord supplied with insufficient information, for example in reference or in accounts, is entitled to withhold consent.

Examples of unreasonable withholding of consent

A refusal of consent is unreasonable where the sole reason is to gain possession, or where the reason is not bona fide, or where the tenant is in breach of repairing covenants and the assignee is prepared to spend a considerable sum on executing repairs. It is not possible to withhold consent on the grounds of race or sex. Generally, it is not possible to withhold consent for reasons outside of the lease.

Remedies for withholding consent

If a tenant is advised that a refusal of consent is unreasonable, or that unreasonable conditions have been imposed on the giving of consent, the tenant can carry out the transaction concerned, risking forfeiture of the lease (loss of lease). The tenant may alternatively apply to the court, usually the county court, for a declaration that the refusal was unreasonable. Where the Landlord and Tenant Act applies and the landlord unreasonably refuses consent, or is deemed to have done so, the tenant may claim damages from the landlord, and any superior landlord.

Remedies of landlord

The landlord may, if he or she could have reasonably withheld consent, provided the lease entitles him to bring an action to forfeit the lease. If in forfeiture proceedings, the court rules that the landlord could not have unreasonably withheld his consent, it has the discretion to grant relief from forfeiture.

****

Chapter 11

Repossession of a Business Lease by a Landlord

When a landlord and tenant enter into a lease, there is a duty by both to observe covenants under the lease. As we have seen, these can be express, implied or statutorily implied covenants. They will bind tenants to pay rent, keep the premises in good repair, pay service charges, not to carry out any alterations, not to cause a nuisance and, usually, not to assign or sublet without the landlord's consent. In addition, there is a binding covenant not to sublet part. These are some of the main tenant's covenants.

The landlord will also be under a duty to observe covenants in the lease, to allow quiet enjoyment and to observe particular repairing covenants, amongst others. There are remedies for both parties when either side does not observe the covenants. If a tenant feels that a landlord's covenant is not being observed then legal advice will be needed before taking any kind of action.

Often, it is the tenant who is faced with repossession and it is the ultimate sanction of repossession which will be outlined below.

A lease will contain a clause, called a forfeiture clause, giving the landlord the right to re-enter, i.e., re-possess the property if the tenant fails to pay the rent within a fixed period (usually 21 days) after the due date, or breaks any of the other obligations or becomes insolvent. However, the landlord does not simply have the right to re-enter a premises. If the landlord wishes to evoke the forfeiture clause, a strict notice procedure must be observed and a court hearing obtained. Until the process has been gone through by the landlord then the tenant has security of tenure. Any unlawful attempts to evict will result in a damages claim against the landlord.

If a business tenant is faced with the threat of forfeiture, then immediate legal advice will be needed, as this is a complicated area and the business tenant has a series of protections before a premises can be repossessed.

****

Chapter 12

Business Leases and Disputes

Often, disputes will arise over one or more elements of the lease and landlord and tenant will have to work out a means of resolving these disputes. Usually, the lease, if well drafted, will contain a mechanism to resolve disputes before the courts intervene. This will often take the form of the appointment of a professional to arbitrate and reach a decision acceptable to both parties. However, if the lease contains no such mechanism, then the courts will have to decide.

It is vital that both landlord and tenant have some idea of the nature of resolving disputes and the facts outlined below are designed to raise awareness of the nature and role of the arbitrator and expert and also the usefulness of informal procedures to avoid the costs associated with the use of professionals.

The two most used alternatives to proceedings in the court are:

Arbitration
Decision by independent expert
One or other of these alternative procedures should be specified for rent reviews that cannot be agreed. They may also be used to settle other problems as well, for example, disputes about service charges or repairs. Awards by arbitrators and determinations by independent experts have some things in common, but in some

respects they are different. The main points of comparison and differences between the two are as follows:

- Arbitrators and experts are appointed, in the first instance, by agreement between landlord and tenant.
- If an appointment cannot be agreed, an appointment is made by an independent person, usually the president of the Royal Institute of Chartered Surveyors.
- An arbitrator is professionally qualified in the subject matter of the dispute and skilled in arbitration law and procedure, whereas the expert is professionally qualified in the subject matter of the dispute with particular knowledge of the type of property and locality.
- An arbitrator is bound to decide the dispute according to the evidence submitted and is not entitled to carry out own investigations and research. The expert, on the other hand is expected to carry out own research. The expert can also disregard any evidence put forward by the landlord or tenant.
- The arbitrator is bound to conduct a hearing, at which both parties are present, if a meeting is requested. The expert need not hold any hearing. An arbitrator must conduct the arbitration in a fair and just manner. The expert must act with due care and diligence but is not bound by the principles of natural justice.
- The arbitrator must ensure that each side has details of the other side's case, and the opportunity to answer it in writing or orally at a hearing.

- An arbitrator will usually give directions at the beginning of a meeting as to how this is to be achieved. The expert has discretion as to whether there should be procedures for the disclosure and rebuttal of any special case advanced by landlord and tenant.
- The arbitrator can order one side or the other to pay all or part of his and the opposing sides costs. The expert cannot order costs unless the lease provides for this.
- The arbitrator may be required to give reasons for his decision. The expert does not have to give reasons.
- A decision by an arbitrator may be the subject of an appeal to the High Court on a point of law under the Arbitration Acts. The decision of an expert is absolutely binding on all questions of fact and law unless clearly outside his terms of reference.
- The arbitrator is probably immune from claims for damages for negligence in the conduct of the reference and his decision. The expert may be liable in damages for professional negligence in carrying out his duties.

Each of these formal procedures can involve landlord and tenant in considerable costs, legal costs and professional fees and expenses. In most cases, the costs can be very significant indeed and if either landlord or tenant is considering evoking the dispute clause, one that involves arbitrators or experts, an attempt should be made to ascertain costs before proceeding. Informal dispute procedures can be a lot more economical although costs will also arise. These are procedures put into train by landlord and tenant which consist of the appointment of an independent person who will attempt to mediate between the two parties in question in order to reach a compromise. The person appointed should be knowledgeable in the area of the dispute, for example rent review and there must be agreement to accept the decision of this person.

****

Chapter 13

Security of Tenure for Business Tenants

The Landlord and Tenant Act 1954 part II

The Landlord and Tenant Act 1954, part II, contains a significant framework of legislation designed to protect tenants of shops, offices, factories, public houses and other business premises. The Act applies in England and Wales but not Scotland.

The Act sets out special rules for both landlord and tenant. The landlord cannot simply evict a tenant following the end of the term of a lease but must follow a strict notice procedure, demonstrating reasonable grounds and the tenant can also follow a strict notice procedure claiming the right to a new tenancy.

When an existing tenancy comes to an end it will continue as a statutory tenancy until the procedures contained within the 1954 Act are exhausted.

Certain notices to be given under the Act by landlords and tenants must be in special form. Each notice has a form number which can be obtained from a legal stationers. The notices are prescribed by the Landlord and Tenant Act 1954, Part 2. New notices were produced as a result of the introduction of the Regulatory Reform (Business Tenancies) (England and Wales) Order 2003, which has introduced simpler regulations designed to assist and protect both landlord and tenant in the process of ending a tenancy.

A useful site to go to, to ascertain which notices to use and also get advice concerning termination of a business lease is https://www.gov.uk/terminating-a-commercial-property-lease-early.

Communities.gov is the site which has superseded the old Office of the Deputy Prime Minister but which still has all the information which is still pertinent. This site has a complete breakdown of all procedures to be adopted when terminating tenancies. Other useful general advice is also available.

The following are facts to be considered when deciding if the procedures prescribed in the Landlord and Tenant Act 1954, part II, apply:

Part II normally applies to any tenant or sub- tenant occupying business premises. A tenant is not covered if he or she has sub-let the whole of the premises and does not occupy them themselves. However, personal occupation by the tenant is not essential, occupation by an agent or manager will suffice.

It will make a difference if the tenancy agreement is in the tenant's name but the tenant trades from the premises as a company. In these circumstances the tenant could lose the right to renew the tenancy. A solicitor should be consulted in this case.

Part II of the Act applies to only a number of types of tenancy. The tenant, who may be an individual or company, may have a lease, or a written or oral tenancy agreement. Certain categories of tenancy are excluded from the Act:

- The tenant of an agricultural holding under a farm business tenancy

- The tenant under a mining lease

- Certain service tenants who were granted their tenancies only because they were employed by their landlord

- A tenant whose tenancy is for a fixed term of six months or less, with no right to renew or extend the tenancy

- Certain tenants who, without the landlords consent, are using the premises for business purposes although prohibited from doing so by the terms of the tenancy

- Tenants holding long leases at low rents which have been extended under the Leasehold Reform Act 1967, and in some cases, sub-tenants of such tenants

- A tenant whose tenancy was granted on the specific understanding that the protection of the Act would not apply, provided that this arrangement was sanctioned in advance by the court.

Licenses are not covered by Part II of the Act. Legal advice needs to be taken in this case.

Agreements excluding security of tenure
It is possible at the outset for landlord and tenant to agree to contract out of the security of tenure provisions under the 1954 Act.

Whereas previously it was necessary to apply to court for approval of an agreement this is no longer the case. However, if an agreement is to be valid it is vital that the parties to the agreement comply fully with either one of two new procedures: the advance notice procedure or the statutory declaration procedure.

The advance notice procedure
The landlord must serve on the tenant a prescribed warning notice at least 14 days before the tenant signs the lease or becomes contractually committed to a lease. Once the 14 days are up the parties are free to sign a lease containing an agreement to exclude security of tenure.

The statutory declaration procedure
It is normally preferable to use the advance notice procedure. This gives the tenant sufficient time to consider whether the exclusion is in their best interests. However, where both parties do not want to wait for the elapse of 14 days, they can make a statutory declaration before an independent solicitor. This is suitable where the tenant wants to occupy the premises quickly.

Details of these procedures and the relevant forms are set out in Schedules 1 and 2 to the Regulatory Reform (Business tenancies) (England and Wales) Order 2003.

The landlord can seek information from the tenant about his or her tenancies or sub tenancies as the lease or tenancy draws to an end. This cannot be sought before there is less than two years of the term left. This must be done by special notice.

The Procedures for terminating and renewing tenancies

By s 24(1) of the Landlord and Tenant Act 1954 Part II, a tenancy to which the Act applies will not come to an end unless terminated in accordance with Part II of the Act. This is the principle of *statutory continuation* of a business tenancy, whether fixed term or periodic. The majority of business leases are covered by the Act.

There are three methods of termination of a business tenancy, to which s 24 will not apply. They are where the tenant gives a notice to quit, in the case of a periodic tenancy, the second is surrender and the third forfeiture. Apart from these methods Part II will apply.

Where the parties agree in writing on a new tenancy, which has the effect of terminating the current tenancy the current tenancy will continue until the commencement date of the new tenancy but Part II will not apply. Part II of the Act provides for various statutory methods of terminating a continuing tenancy by means of statutory notices, as follows:

The tenant has the right to terminate a fixed term tenancy, on it coming to an end, prior to the start of continuation under Part II, by notice under s 27.

The landlord has the right to terminate a fixed term or periodic tenancy by notice in the prescribed form under s 25.

The tenant may request a new tenancy under s 26 by a notice in the prescribed form, where the current tenancy is a fixed term tenancy exceeding one year, continued by s 24(1) or not. In the case of fixed terms for less than one year and periodic tenancies, the tenant cannot request a new tenancy under s 26 unless he is given a landlord's s 25 notice.

Termination of a fixed term tenancy by the tenant under s 27

A tenancy for a fixed term will be continued beyond its contractual term date automatically under s 24 of the Landlord and Tenant Act 1954 Part II, unless steps are taken to prevent it by the tenant under s 27(1) or by the landlord under s 25. A tenant is required to give the landlord not less than three months notice that he does not want it to continue. Alternatively, a tenant can terminate a tenancy that is continuing after time, under s 27(2) by giving not less than three months notice in writing expiring on any quarter day.

No special form of notice is required but, in neither case, can the notice validly be given by the tenant until he has been in occupation for more than one month. Once notice is validly given the tenant will lose any rights under the act and the tenancy will terminate on the date specified.

Termination of the tenancy by the landlord under s 25

A landlord's only way to terminate a tenancy to which Part II applies, other than by granting a new tenancy or forfeiture, is by giving the tenant a notice to terminate under s 25 of Part II of the Act. This applies to all periodic tenancies and tenancies for a fixed term exceeding six months whether or not they are continuing under s 24 (1). The landlord's notice must comply strictly with the provisions of the Act. These are as follows:

Form. The notice must be in writing, in the prescribed form or in a substantially similar form. All particulars must be correct.

Date of termination. The notice must specify the date on which the current tenancy is to come to an end. The date specified must not be earlier than the date on which, in the case of a fixed term tenancy, it would have expired by effluxion of time. In the case of a periodic tenancy, it must not be earlier than the earliest date on which the current tenancy could have been brought to an end by a notice to quit served by the landlord.

Giving a s 25 notice. A s25 notice may be given by the landlord not less than six, nor more than 12 months before the termination date specified in the notice. The notice must be served by the landlord. A landlord may terminate at one and the same time the tenancy and any sub tenancies derived out of it.

A tenants counter notice

The landlord's notice must require the tenant to notify the landlord in writing whether or not, at the date of termination specified in the landlords notice, he will be willing to give up possession. This provides in effect, for the serving of a counter notice by the tenant. The notice need not be in any special form. The 2003 Regulations have removed the time frame for the counter notice as a lot of tenants were falling foul of this.

The landlords notice must, under s 25(6) of the Act state whether or not the landlord would oppose the application to the court by the tenant for a new tenancy and if so, on what grounds he will rely. The grounds on which a landlord can oppose an application for a new tenancy are as follows:

That the tenant ought not to have a new tenancy because he has not sufficiently complied with the terms of his current tenancy or has otherwise failed to behave properly as a tenant (paragraphs (a) to (c))

That the landlord can provide suitable alternative accommodation for the tenant. Paragraph (d)

That the application for a new tenancy is made by a sub-tenant occupying part of the premises, that the landlord is in a position to let or sell the premises as a whole, and that he ought to get possession of the part occupied by the sub tenant since otherwise he will suffer substantial loss. Paragraph (e)

That the landlord requires possession in order to demolish or reconstruct the premises. Paragraph (f)

That the landlord intends to occupy the premises himself for business purposes or as his residence. The landlord cannot use this ground if he bought the premises over the head of the sitting tenant less than five years before the end of the tenancy. Paragraph (g)

The grounds are laid out in full a little further on. The landlord who relies on suitable alternative accommodation may fail to satisfy the court that the alternative accommodation will be immediately available at the end of the current tenancy. But if he shows that it will be available up to 12 months later, the court will not grant a new tenancy and may within the 14 days time limit under the act, if the tenant requires, extend the current tenancy until the later date.

The same happens if the landlord relies on paragraphs (e) or (f) and can show that he needs possession up to 12 months later than the end of the current tenancy.

A landlord who relies on paragraph (f) will not succeed if: The tenant agrees to a new tenancy giving the landlord access enabling him/her to carry out the intended work, which would not substantially interfere with the tenant's work.

OR

The tenant agrees to accept a new tenancy of an economically separate part of the premises and either:

- This new tenancy gives the landlord access to enable him to carry out the intended work which would not substantially interfere with the tenant's business with respect to that part or

- Possession of the remainder of the premises by the landlord would be reasonably sufficient to enable the landlord to carry out the intended work.

Application to the court

The tenant must apply not earlier than two months but not later than four months after requesting a new tenancy, or after the notice of termination is given to him. If he/she does not apply within this period he/she will lose the rights to do so and to stay in the premises. Unless a tenant has been able to reach a binding agreement with the landlord in writing on all the terms of a new tenancy before the end of the two-to-four-month period the tenant will always have to apply to the court to protect his/her position.

Provided that the tenant observes the time limits for applying, the court *must* order a new tenancy to be granted unless the landlord can prove a ground summarized previously and outlined in full below.

If the landlord can satisfy the court that he is entitled to possession of the property on one or more grounds then the court *must* grant him possession. If the landlord cannot do so then the court *must* order the grant of a new tenancy.

The application for a new tenancy will be to the local county court, although the High Court can deal with more complex issues. The terms of the new tenancy can be those agreed in writing between the landlord and tenant or can be determined by the court, regarding the current tenancy.

If the grant of a new tenancy is refused, compensation is payable on the tenant quitting the premises, but only if:

The landlord has opposed or the court has refused the grant of a new tenancy solely on the grounds set out in paragraph (e) (f) or (g) as shown below.

There is no agreement, which effectively excludes compensation.

Landlord's grounds for opposing an application for a new tenancy

As we have seen, if the tenant applies to the court for a new tenancy, the landlord can only oppose the application on one or more grounds set out in s 30(1) of the 1954 Act. Although mentioned briefly above, the grounds are fully outlined below.

The paragraph letters are those used in the Act. The landlord can only use a ground if the paragraph letter is shown in paragraph 5 of the notice given in the special form. The Grounds are as follows-

- where under the current tenancy the tenant has any obligations with respect to the repair and maintenance of the holding, that the tenant ought not to be granted a new tenancy in view of the state of the holding, being a state resulting from the tenant's failure to comply with the said obligations.
- -that the tenant ought not to be granted a new tenancy in view of his persistent delay in paying rent and other charges that the tenant ought not to be granted a new tenancy in view of
- other substantial breaches by him of his other obligations under the current tenancy or for any other reason connected with the tenants use or management of his holding.
- -that the landlord has offered or is willing to provide or secure the provision of suitable alternative accommodation for the tenant, that the terms on which the alternative accommodation is available are reasonable having regards to the terms of the current tenancy and to all other relevant circumstances, and that the accommodation and the time at which it will be available are suitable for the tenants

requirements (including the requirement to preserve goodwill) having regard to the nature and class of his business and to the situation and extent of, and facilities afforded by, the holding;
- -where the current tenancy was created by the subletting of part only of the property comprised in a superior tenancy and the landlord is the owner of an interest in reversion expectant on the termination of that superior tenancy, that the aggregate of the rents reasonably obtainable on separate lettings of the holding, and the remainder of that property would be substantially less than the rent reasonably obtainable on a letting of that property as a whole, that on the termination of the current tenancy the landlord requires possession of the holding for the purposes of letting or otherwise disposing of the said property as a whole, and that in view thereof the tenant ought not to be granted a new tenancy;
- -that on the termination of the current tenancy the landlord intends to demolish or reconstruct the premises comprised in the holding or a substantial part of those premises or to carry out substantial work of construction on the holding or part thereof and that he could not reasonably do so without obtaining possession of the holding.
- (If the landlord uses this ground, the court can still sometimes grant a new tenancy if certain conditions set out in s 31(A) of the Act can be met)
- -that on the termination of the current tenancy the landlord intends to occupy the holding for the purposes, or partly for

the purposes, of a business to be carried out by him herein, or as his residence. The landlord must normally have been the landlord for more than five years to use this ground.

The amount of compensation the tenant receives depends on how long the tenant has been in occupation carrying on a business in the premises. If it has been less than 14 years the tenant receives a sum equal to the appropriate multiplier (see below) times the rateable value of the property occupied at the end of the tenancy.

For 14 years or more the tenant will receive the appropriate multiplier time twice the rateable value of the property occupied at the end of the tenancy.

Since 1st April 1990 the appropriate multiplier has been prescribed by the Landlord and Tenant Act 1954 (Appropriate Multiplier) Order 1990 (S1 1990 no 363). This order prescribes a multiplier of:

Where the date for determining the rateable value is on or after 1st April 1990 (If part of the property is domestic this will be disregarded in determining the rateable value. If the tenant occupies on the date a section 25 or s 26 (6) notice under the 1954 Landlord and tenant Act is served, the whole or any part of the domestic property, he will also be entitled to a sum equal to his reasonable expenses in removing from the domestic property.

If the landlords notice was served before 1st April 1990, and so the date for determining the rateable value is before that date, but the tenant quits on or after 1st April 1990.

For some tenancies existing or contracted for, before 1st April 1990 where the tenant has opted for compensation to be based on the rateable value of the holding on 31st March 1990 during a transitional period (i.e. where the landlords s 25 notice is given after the 31st March 1990 but before 1st April 2000) as set out in schedule seven to the Local Government and Housing Act 1989. The tenant must opt not less than two nor more than four months after the landlords notice or after he has requested a new tenancy.

Professional advice may be needed on which of the three multipliers is the appropriate one in individual cases and, for example, concerning any queries about the rateable value. tenant may also be entitled to compensation under other Acts. If in doubt seek professional advice.

It is extremely important that all business tenants/lessees are aware of their rights when nearing the end of their tenancy/lease term. In all likelihood, it will probably be necessary to obtain legal advice if tenants/lessees intend to renew a tenancy or make an application to a court for renewal and the landlord intends to oppose on the grounds laid out above. This should be sought as soon as possible.

In many cases, if a tenant has a good track record and a business is successful then the granting of a new lease/tenancy is a formality. However, for a number of reasons, the landlord may wish to get back his premises. Approaches to the landlord should be made well in advance in order to determine the situation regarding the granting of a tenancy.

****

Conclusion

As this book has shown, the investor, or potential investor, in commercial property, needs a lot of background knowledge before succeeding in building up a viable portfolio of properties which provide an income and an increase in capital value. the commercial property market is far more complex than the residential buy-to-let market. In addition, the advent of the coronavirus on the investment landscape was significant, and more and more people left offices to work from home. Now, at the time of writing, we have an inflationary environment which makes investment risky. Therefore, any would be investor needs to take into account the impact of the virus and all its manifestations before moving forward.

The investor needs a general knowledge of the market along with knowledge of the potential investment vehicles, including pension funds. In addition, access to finance for commercial properties is different and more complicated than for residential property, although the basics might be the same.

A knowledge of the planning system is essential if buying a property that has potential for conversion. Also, an idea of how to source properties at auction is useful. This runs hand in hand with a knowledge of the planning process.

Finally, as Part 2 of the book demonstrates, a knowledge of the legislative environment surrounding the management of commercial properties is vital. You may have bought the freehold of a premises that includes a shop or is a shop alone. You will receive the rent from these commercial premises but at some point, you will need to understand the law and practice of management.

A comprehensive commercial property portfolio can consist of assets such as shops and offices, it can also comprise investments through commercial property funds. The main areas to help and assist you in this process are clearly laid out in this brief but comprehensive book.

****

Useful Addresses, Contacts and Publications.

Property advice

The Royal Institute of Chartered Surveyors (RICS) Information Centre on 020 7686 8555 www.rics.org.uk.

The RICS also supply, free of charge "Rent Review – a guide for small businesses" send a large stamped, self addressed envelope to Corporate Communications, The Royal Institute of Chartered Surveyors, RICS Contact Centre, Surveyor Court, Westwood way, Coventry CV4 8JE.

The Property Managers Association, through Boots the Chemist also provides a guide to good practice on service charges in commercial property. Contact:

The Property Managers Association
The Dolls House, Audley End Business Centre
Saffron Walden, Essex, CB11 4JL
Phone: 01799 544904
Fax: 01799 542991 Email: admin@srevents.co.uk

The RICS publish a code of practice for commercial property leases in England and Wales, obtainable from the address above.

For information on local solicitors who could represent you, call the Law Society on 0207 242 1222. www.lawsociety.org.uk.

Property owners' association
The trade association which looks after the interests of property owners is:
The British Property Federation,
5th Floor
St Albans House
57-59 Haymarket
London SW1Y 4QX
Tel: 020 7828 0111
Fax: 020 7834 3442
Email: info@bpf.org.uk

Useful Addresses
British Council for Offices
78-79 Leadenhall Street
London
EC3A 3DH
Tel: 020 7283 0125
Fax: 020 7626 1553
Email: mail@bco.org.uk

British Retail Consortium
Second Floor 21 Dartmouth Street
London SW1H 9BP
Tel: 020 7854 8900 Email events@brs.org.uk

Federation of Small Businesses
Sir Frank Whittle Way

Blackpool Business Park
Blackpool
Lancs
FY4 2FE www.fsb.org.uk
Tel: 0808 20 20 888

****

Index

Acts of God, 98
Agreements excluding security of tenure, 121
Amenity Land, 71
Arbitration, 115, 117
Assignee, 88
Assignment, 3, 109, 110
Assignor, 88
Assured shorthold tenancy agreements, 28

Bricks and mortar funds, 35
British Property Federation, 7, 136
Building Land, 70
Business Leases, 87
Buying costs, 25
Buy-to-let investors, 69

Capital values, 31
Commercial Investments, 70
Commercial property funds, 35
Commonholds, 17
Consultation, 105
Contract for a lease, 91
Coronavirus, 5
Covenant Strength, 32

Damp, 78
Demised premises, 88
Department stores, 12
Depreciation, 15
Developers, 68
Development Propositions, 69
Disputes, 103, 115
Distribution warehousing, 12

Electrics and plumbing, 77
Energy performance, 6
Essential Information Group, 72, 73
Estates Gazette, 6, 72
Estimated budget expenditure, 105
Express covenants, 93

Financial Conduct Authority, 37
Flipping, 68
Forced sales, 69
Freehold property, 17
Full repairing and insurance leases, 96

Garage blocks, 70
Ground rents, 69

High Court, 117, 128

Implied covenants, 93
Industrial units, 70
Insurance, 98, 99
Investment properties, 69

Landlord and Tenant Act 1954, 4, 89, 119, 120, 123, 124, 131, 141, 167
Landlord and Tenant Act 1954 (Appropriate Multiplier) Order 1990 (SI 1990 no 363), 131
Landlord and Tenant Acts 1985/1987 and 1996, 101, 105
Landlord's covenants, 92
Landlord's grounds for opposing an application for a new tenancy, 128
Leasehold property, 17
Local authority properties, 69
Local Government and Housing Act 1989, 132
Logistical facilities, 12

Market risks, 16
Minimum base rent, 95
Mixed Use Properties, 70

Office of Deputy Prime Minister, 122
Open Ended Investment Companies, 37
Open Market Value, 95

Preliminary negotiations, 91
Private investors, 12
Privity of contract, 18
Probates, 69
Properties for Improvement, 69
Property advisors, 95
Property auction, 67
Property Auction News, 71
Property investment trusts, 38
Property investors, 68
Property surveys, 77
Provision of certified accounts, 106
Real Estate Investment Trusts (REITs, 37
Receivership sales, 69
Regulatory reform (Business Tenancies) (England and Wales) Order 2003, 119
Rent, 94, 101, 135, 143, 146, 147, 154, 155, 160, 161, 163, 164, 165, 167, 168, 169, 170, 171, 173
Rent reviews, 18
Repairs, 97
Repossession, 3, 113
Repossessions, 69
Retail shops, 70
Retail warehouses, 12
Return on investment (ROI, 30
Right to renew, 97

Security of Tenure, 4, 119
Self-Invested Personal Pension Plan (SIPP), 39
Service charge apportionments, 103
Service charges, 101, 103
Service Charges, 101
Shopping centres, 12
Sinking funds, 108
Stamp Duty Land Tax, 25
Statutorily implied covenants, 93
Structure of the building, 78
Student accommodation, 12
Sub lease, 89
Subletting, 109
Supermarkets, 12

Tax, 45
Tenants counter notice, 125
Termination of a business tenancy, 123
Termination of a fixed term tenancy, 124
Termination of the tenancy by the landlord, 124
The advance notice procedure, 122
The Royal Institute of Chartered Surveyors (RICS), 135
The statutory declaration procedure, 122
Turnover rent, 95

Unique Properties, 70
Unsold property, 82
Use of premises, 99

Value for money, 103
VAT, 25
Viewing, 75
Viewing an auction property, 75

Withdrawn property, 83

Yield, 30, 31, 32

Zero-carbon Building methods, 7

****

Appendix 1
Forms and their purposes under the Landlord and Tenant Act 1954 Part 2

Form number	Purpose
1	Ending a tenancy, where the landlord is not opposed to the grant of a new one
2	Ending a tenancy, where the landlord is opposed to the grant of a new one
3	Tenants request for a new tenancy of a premises
4	Landlords request for information from the tenant
5	Tenants request for information from the landlord or the landlords mortgage lender
6	Withdrawal of notice given under s 25 of the act ending a tenancy
7	Ending a tenancy, where the landlord is opposed to the grant of a new tenancy but where the tenant may be entitled under the 1967 Act to buy the freehold or extend the lease
8	Ending a tenancy, where a certificate given under section 57 of the act that the use or occupation or part of it is to be changed by a specified date
9	Ending a tenancy where a certificate given under section 57 of the Act that the use or occupation of the property or part of it is to be changed at a future date and the landlord opposes granting a new tenancy
10	Ending a tenancy to which Part 2 of the act applies, where a certificate given under section 57 of the act that the use or occupation of the property is to be changed at a future date and the landlord does not oppose granting a new tenancy

11	Ending a tenancy, where a certificate given under section 58 of the Act that for reasons of national security it is necessary that the use or occupation of the property should be discontinued or changed
12	Ending a tenancy, where a certificate given under section 60 of the Act that it is necessary or expedient for regeneration purposes that the use or occupation of the property should be changed.

Appendix 2

Sample business lease – mixed commercial/rented premises (shop with flat above)

PARTICULARS

Date of Lease	20
The Parties	1. The Landlord
	2. The Tenant
The Premises	Shown edged red on the attached plan
The Rent	The yearly rent of £6,000.00 or such higher sum as may be payable under clause 6 of this lease.
The Term	12 years from 20
The Permitted Use	1. As to the ground floor shop use as a shop within Class A1 in the Schedule to the Town and Country Planning (Use Classes) Order 1 987 for the trade or business of the sale of fishing tackle and ancillary merchandise or for such other trade or business not prohibited by this lease as shall be approved by the Landlord in writing (such approval not to be unreasonably withheld) 2. As to the first and second floor maisonette use as a private residence in the occupation of a single family

| The Review Dates | 2023 2028 and the day before the expiry of the period referred to in the above definition of "the Term" |

THIS LEASE is made between the Parties referred to in the foregoing particulars.

1. IN this lease unless the context otherwise requires: -

(1) The expression "the Particulars" shall mean the foregoing particulars

(2) The expressions contained in the Particulars shall have the respective meanings assigned to them in the Particulars

(3) The expression "the Landlord" shall include the person persons or corporation for the time being entitled to the reversion immediately expectant on the termination of the Term

(4) The expression "the Tenant" shall include the successors in title of the Tenant

(5) The expression "the Term" shall include the period of any holding over or extension continuance or renewal thereof whether by statute common law or agreement

(6) The expression "the Insured Risks" shall mean the risks of fire explosion lightning impact flood storm or tempest riot or civil commotion bursting or overflowing of water tanks apparatus or pipes boilers heating plant and equipment or such of them and any other risks against which the Landlord may reasonably consider it necessary or desirable and be able to insure

(7) The expression "the Granted Rights" shall mean the right for the Tenant in common with all other persons having the like right from time to time and at all times to pass and repass over and along the passageway shown hatched blue on the attached plan and the right of passage and running of water and soil from the Premises through the sewers or drains running under the said passageway and to enter upon such passageway for the purpose of repairing cleansing and maintaining such sewers or drains the Tenant making good all damage occasioned thereby

(8) The expression "the Reserved Rights" shall mean: -

(a) The right to use any pipes wires drains sewers gutters cables ducts and other conducting media plant equipment and installations supplying any adjoining premises belonging to the Landlord with services and passing through under or over or being in the Premises and the right to enter the Premises for the purpose of maintaining and repairing such pipes wires drains sewers gutters cables ducts and other conducting media the person exercising such right causing as little damage or disturbance as possible and making good all damage actually caused to the Premises as the result or in the course of any such entry

(b) The right to enter upon the Premises for the purposes (or any of them) referred to and in accordance with the provisions of this lease

(9) The expression "the Planning Acts" shall mean the Town and Country Planning Act 1990 The Planning (Listed Buildings and Conservation Areas) Act 1990 The Planning (Hazardous Substances) Act 1990 the Planning (Consequential Provisions) Act 1990 as from time to time modified or re-enacted and any regulations or orders made under the authority of any such Act

(10) The expression "Enactment" shall mean an Act of Parliament statutory instrument order or byelaw for the time being in force and shall include any rule regulation scheme plan or direction issued under or deriving authority from any such act instrument order or byelaw and a reference to a particular Enactment shall be deemed to refer to that Enactment as from time to time modified re-enacted or replaced

(11) The singular shall include the plural the masculine shall include the feminine and the neuter and covenants entered into and burdens assumed by a party consisting of more than one person shall be deemed to be entered into and assumed jointly and severally so as to apply to and be enforceable against all both or any of such persons and their and each of their personal representatives

---

2. THE Landlord demises to the Tenant the Premises and the Landlord's fixtures and fittings in the Premises TOGETHER with the Granted Rights but EXCEPT AND RESERVING to the Landlord and the tenant or tenants for the time being of any adjoining premises belonging to the Landlord the Reserved Rights for the Term YIELDING AND PAYING

(1) The Rent which shall be paid by equal quarterly instalments in advance on the usual quarter days the first of such instalments being calculated proportionately from the..........................20 to the next following quarter day having already been paid such payments to be made so long as the Landlord shall not otherwise require by bankers standing order

(2) By way of further rent on demand 'all sums payable by the Tenant to the Landlord under the provisions of this lease

3. THE Tenant covenants with the Landlord throughout the Term:-

(1) To pay the Rent without any deduction or abatement whatsoever except only such sums as are by law payable by the Landlord to the exclusion of the Tenant notwithstanding any stipulation to the contrary

(2) To pay to the Landlord from time to time on demand

    (a)
A sum or sums equal to such amount or amounts as shall from time to time be expended by the Landlord in insuring the Premises and the Landlord's fixtures and fittings therein of an insurable nature against the Insured Risks and all boilers and heating apparatus therein and plant used in connection with such boilers against the risk of explosion and in effecting or maintaining insurance in such sum or sums as the Landlord shall think fit indemnifying the Landlord against third party and property owner's risks in respect of the Premises and any liability which the Landlord may incur by reason of the condition of the Premises whether under the Defective Premises Act 1 972 or otherwise or (if any such sum or sums shall relate to the insurance of other premises as well as the Premises) the proportion of such sum or sums attributable to the Premises such proportion to be fixed by the Landlord or his surveyor or agent whose decision shall be final

    (b)
Such sum as shall from time to time be expended by the Landlord i insuring or causing to be insured the Premises against loss of the Rent for a period of three years taking into account any potential increase in the Rent under the provisions of this lease.

(3) To pay or repay to the Landlord and discharge all rates taxes duties charges assessments impositions and outgoings whether

parliamentary parochial local or of any other description save for any tax payable on or as a result of any disposal of or dealing with the Landlord and all charges for gas electricity telephone water sewage and other services which are now or may at any time hereafter be taxed charged or imposed upon or payable in respect of the Premises or on the owner or occupier of the Premises and not to leave the Premises or permit the Premises to be left unused or unoccupied nor to claim or permit to be claimed void rating relief in respect of the Premises if as a result the Landlord will be deprived from claiming such relief for any period after the determination of the Term

(4)

(a)   To put maintain and keep the whole of the Premises and all additions and improvements and the Landlord's fixtures and fittings in the Premises and all appurtenances forming part of the Premises in good and tenantable repair and decorative order in every respect (damage by any of the Insured Risks only excepted save to the extent to which the payment of a claim by the Landlord is refused by the insurers in whole or in part as the result of any act neglect or default of the Tenant or any sub-tenant or any licensee servant or agent of the Tenant or any sub-tenant) PROVIDED that the Tenant shall not be required to put maintain or keep the Premises in a better state of repair than the state at the date of this lease as evidenced by the attached schedule of condition

(b)   When and so often as any Landlord's fixtures shall reasonably require replacement to substitute other fixtures of a similar description quality and value to the reasonable satisfaction of the Landlord

(c)   To keep all external parts (if any) of the Premises clean and tidy and all landscaped areas (if any) forming part of the Premises in a proper state of cultivation and to replace any trees shrubs or plants therein which may die or become affected by disease

(5)   Whenever required by the Landlord to pay or contribute a fair proportion attributable to the Premises of the cost and expense of repairing maintaining renewing rebuilding lighting and cleansing any yards passages forecourts pipes wires drains sewers gutters cables ducts and other conducting media plant equipment and installations fences roofs walls or other appurtenances or conveniences which shall belong to or be used by or for the Premises, in common with other nearby or adjoining premises (such proper proportion to be certified by the Landlord's surveyors)

(6)   In every third year computed from the commencement of the Term and also in the last six months of the Term (whether determined by effluxion of time or otherwise) provided that in such circumstances there shall not be an obligation arising twice in 1 2 months to prepare and paint with three coats of paint of good quality or otherwise treat as the case may require all external parts of the Premises which have previously been or usually are or ought to be or require to be painted or otherwise treated respectively in tints or colours to be approved in writing by the Landlord such approval not to be unreasonably withheld or delayed and also as often as in the Landlord's opinion shall be necessary to clean wash down point make good and restore the exterior stone or brick work and other finishes of the exterior of the Premises and restore the same to their former condition and appearance to the reasonable satisfaction of the Landlord and in every fifth year computed from the commencement of the Term and also in the last six months of the Term (whether determined by effluxion of time or otherwise) provided that in such circumstances there shall not be an obligation arising twice in 1 2 months to prepare and paint with two coats of paint of good quality redecorate or paper with paper of good quality or otherwise treat as the case may be all internal parts of the Premises which have previously been or usually are or ought to

be so painted decorated papered or treated (the tints colours and patterns in respect of the work done in the last six months of the Term to be approved in writing by the Landlord) such consent not to be unreasonably withheld or delayed and to wash down all tiles glazed bricks and similar washable surfaces all such works to be carried out in a good and workmanlike manner

(7)   Not to do or permit to be done any act or thing which may obstruct or damage the drainage system of the Premises or any part thereof nor to deposit or permit the escape of trade effluent or other obnoxious or deleterious materials into such drainage system

(8)   At the expiration or sooner determination of the Term peaceably and quietly to yield up the Premises and the Landlord's fixtures and fittings in the Premises together with all additions and improvements to the Landlord in such state and condition as shall in all respects be consistent with due performance by the Tenant of the covenants contained in this lease and if so required by the Landlord to remove all or any trade or tenant's fixtures removable by the Tenant and all partitioning or other alterations installed or effected by the Tenant with or without the Landlord's approval and to make good to the Landlord's reasonable satisfaction all damage to the Premises caused or revealed by such removal

(9)   To observe and comply in all respects with all and any provisions requirements and directions of or under any Enactment so far as they or it shall relate to or affect the Premises or any fixture machinery plant or chattel for the time being in the Premises or the use of the Premises for the purpose of any trade or business or the employment in the Premises of any person or persons or the supply to the Premises of any service and to execute all works which by or under any Enactment or by any government department local authority

factory inspector statutory undertaker or other public authority or duly authorized officer or court of competent jurisdiction acting under or in pursuance of any Enactment are or may be directed or required to be executed whether by the Landlord or by the Tenant at any time during the Term upon or in respect of the Premises or any such fixture machinery plant or chattel or in respect of any such use employment or supply and to indemnify the Landlord at all times against all costs charges and expenses of or incidental to the execution of any such works and not at any time during the Term to do or omit or suffer to be done or omitted on or about the Premises any act or thing in breach of the terms of this lease by reason of which the Landlord may under any Enactment incur or have imposed upon him or become liable to pay any penalty damages compensation costs charges or expenses

(10) To give full particulars to the Landlord of any permission notice order direction or proposal for a notice order or direction made given or issued to the Tenant by any government department local or public authority under or by virtue of any Enactment within 14 days of the receipt by the Tenant of notice of the same and if so required by the Landlord to produce such permission notice order or direction or proposal for a notice order or direction to the Landlord AND ALSO without delay to take all reasonable or necessary steps to comply with any such notice order or direction and also at the request of the Landlord to make or join with the Landlord in making such objections or representations against or in respect of any such notice order proposal or direction as the Landlord shall deem expedient

(11) To notify the Landlord forthwith in writing of any defect in or want of repair for which the Landlord may be responsible to third parties under the Defective Premises Act 1 972 or any other Enactment and to indemnify the Landlord against all

liability and expense which may be sustained or incurred by the Landlord in respect of any notice claim or demand costs and proceedings made or brought under such Act or other Enactment Or as a result of any failure by the Tenant to give any such notification

(12)   In relation to the Planning Acts: -

(a)   To comply in all respects with the provisions and requirements of the Planning Acts relating to the Premises and the use of the Premises and all licences consents permissions and conditions granted to the Tenant or imposed on the Tenant or the Premises under the Planning Acts relating to or affecting the Premises or any part of the Premises or any operations works acts or things already or to be carried out executed done or omitted on the Premises or the use of the Premises for any purpose

(b)   So often as occasion shall require at the expense in all respects of the Tenant to obtain from (as the case may be) the local planning authority or the appropriate government department all such Licenses consents and permissions as may be required from the carrying out by the Tenant of any operations on the Premises or the institution or continuance by the Tenant on the Premises of any use which may constitute development within the meaning of the Planning Acts

To pay and satisfy any charge that may at any time be imposed under the Planning Acts in respect of the carrying out or maintenance by the

tenant on the Premises of any such operations or the institution or continuance by the Tenant of any such use

(d)   Notwithstanding any consent which may be granted by the Landlord under this lease not to carry out or make any alteration or addition to or change of use of the Premises being an alteration or addition or change of use for which planning permission under the Planning Acts needs to be obtained or carry out any development (as defined by the Planning Acts) on or to the Premises without first obtaining such planning permission and not to apply for any such planning permission without first obtaining the Landlord's approval in writing which shall be deemed to lapse if such planning permission shall not be granted within six months of the date of the Landlord's approval

(e)   Unless the Landlord shall otherwise direct to carry out before the expiration or sooner determination of the Term any works stipulated to be carried out to the Premises by a date subsequent to such expiration or sooner determination as a condition of any licence consent or permission which may have been granted during the Term

(f)   To indemnify and keep indemnified the Landlord against any liability resulting from any contravention of the provisions of the Planning Acts

(13)   To permit the Landlord and the owner or tenant of any adjoining premises and his or their surveyors or agents with or without workmen and others at all reasonable hours during the daytime on reasonable written notice being given (except in emergency) to enter (and in emergency to break and enter) the Premises or any part of the Premises for the purposes of inspecting and executing repairs or alterations to such adjoining premises or the pipes wires drains sewers gutters cables ducts and other conducting media plant equipment and installations in the Premises supplying such adjoining premises with services and for such purpose to erect and maintain scaffolding and machinery and deposit materials on any suitable part of the Premises the person so entering the Premises causing as little damage or disturbance as possible and making good in a

reasonable manner all damage actually caused to the Premises in the course or as a result of any such entry

(14)   To permit the Landlord and his surveyor or agent with or without workmen and others at all reasonable hours during the daytime on reasonable written notice being given (except in emergency) to enter the Premises or any part of the Premises to ensure that nothing has been done in the Premises that constitutes a breach of any of the Tenant's covenants contained in this lease or to view and examine the state and condition of the Premises or to take inventories of the fixtures and fittings in the Premises or to make any inspection for the purposes of the Landlord and Tenant Acts 1 927 and 1 954 or any other Enactment for the time being affecting the Premises or any review of the Rent or any renewal (whether statutory or otherwise) of this lease as often as occasion shall require the person so entering the Premises causing as little damage and disturbance as possible and making good in a reasonable manner any damage actually caused to the Premises in the course or as a result of any such entry

(15)   To permit any independent surveyor or arbitrator who may be appointed for the purpose of any review of the Rent under the provisions contained in this lease to enter the Premises in order to inspect the same and to supply to him such information as he shall properly require

(16)   To repair and make good all breaches of covenant defects and wants of repair or decoration for which the Tenant may be liable under the covenants contained in this lease of which notice shall have been given by the Landlord to the Tenant within two calendar months after the giving of such notice or sooner if requisite AND if the Tenant shall at any time make default in the performance of this covenant it shall be lawful for (but not obligatory upon) the Landlord (but without prejudice to his right of

re-entry or any other right or remedy available to the Landlord under this lease or otherwise) to enter upon the Premises and to carry out and execute such works as may be required to repair and redecorate the Premises in accordance with such covenants and to repay to the Landlord forthwith on demand all expenses (including any legal costs surveyors fees and other similar expenses) incurred by the Landlord in respect of such works

(17)   To permit the Landlord or his agents at any time (in the case of a proposed sale of the Landlord's interest in the Premises) or within six calendar months next before the expiration or sooner determination of the Term to enter upon the Premises and to fix and retain without interference upon any suitable part or parts of the Premises a notice board or notice boards for reletting or selling the Premises and not to remove or obscure such board or boards and on reasonable written notice to permit all persons by order in writing of the Landlord or his agents to view the Premises at all convenient hours in the daytime without interruption

(18)   To pay to the Landlord all reasonable costs charges and expenses (including legal costs and fees payable to a surveyor or architect) which may be incurred or payable by the Landlord in or in contemplation of any steps taken to recover any arrears of the Rent or the enforcement of any of the covenants contained in this lease or the preparation and service of all notices and schedules relating to wants of repair to the Premises and agreeing such schedules with the Tenant whether before at or within 3 months after the termination of the Term or any proceedings relating to the Premises or the preparation and service of a notice under section 146 or 147 of the Law of Property Act 1 925 (whether or not any right of re-entry or forfeiture has been waived by the Landlord or the Tenant has been relieved under the provisions of such Act) or as a result or in contemplation of any application to any planning authority or

of any application to the Landlord for any licence or consent pursuant to the covenants contained in this lease or in respect of any improvement which the Tenant may be entitled to make on or to the Premises under or by virtue of the Landlord and Tenant Acts 1927 and 1 954 or any other Enactment for the time being affecting the Premises or in connection with the approval from time to time of any such works and to keep the Landlord fully and effectually indemnified against all liability which he may incur in respect of any such application licence consent or works

(19)   Not to place bring keep or deposit on the Premises any article or substance in such position or in such quantity or weight as to exceed the load bearing capabilities of the ceilings roofs walls floor members or structure of the Premises and not to do anything which may endanger the safety or stability of the Premises or any neighbouring or adjoining premises

(20)   Not to keep place or store or permit or suffer to be kept placed or stored in or upon or about the Premises any substance liquid or gas of a dangerous offensive combustible inflammable radioactive or explosive or corrosive nature or the keeping or storing of which may contravene any Enactment or require the licence or consent of any local or other competent authority or constitute a nuisance to the occupiers of neighbouring or adjoining premises

(21)   (a)   Not to do or omit or suffer to be done or omitted any act matter or thing whatsoever the doing or omission of which would make void or voidable any policy of insurance of the Premises or any part thereof or any neighbouring or adjoining premises or cause the premium payable in respect of any such insurance to be increased above the normal rate

(b)   In the event of the Premises or any part of the Premises or any fixture or fitting in the Premises insured by the Landlord being destroyed or damaged by any of the Insured Risks to give immediate notice to the Landlord

(c)   In the event of the Premises or any part of the Premises or any fixture or fitting in the Premises insured by the Landlord being destroyed or damaged by any of the Insured Risks and the insurance money under any policy of insurance effected by the Landlord being wholly or partly irrecoverable by reason of any act or default of the Tenant or any sub-tenant or any licensee servant or agent of the Tenant or any sub-tenant or by reason of any excess applied by the insurers forthwith to pay to the Landlord the whole or (as the case may require) the irrecoverable part of the cost of rebuilding reinstating or repairing the Premises. as the case may be or replacing or repairing such fixture or fitting

(22)   To take all reasonable precautions against the outbreak of fire on the Premises and in particular to provide and keep in good repair and condition any fire alarms fire escapes and fire fighting or fire preventive equipment which shall be required to be kept in the Premises by any competent authority or by the Landlord

(23)   Not at any time to make any alteration or addition to the electrical installation of the Premises save in accordance with the terms and conditions laid down by the Institution of Electrical Engineers and the regulations of the electricity supply authority

(24)   (a)   Not to make any structural alteration or addition whatsoever to or on the Premises
(b)   Not without the previous consent in writing of the Landlord (such consent if granted to be without prejudice nevertheless to the provisions of sub-clause (12) of this clause) nor except in accordance with plans and specifications previously submitted to and approved by the Landlord's architects or surveyors to make

any other addition or alteration to the Premises (including conducting media plant equipment and installations therein for the supply of services) such consent not to be unreasonably withheld

(25) Not to use or permit to be used the Premises except for the Permitted Use and in particular not at any time to use the Premises or permit the Premises to be used for any illegal or immoral purpose or for any purpose which may infringe any legislation for the time being in force or for any noisy noxious dangerous or offensive trade business manufacture or occupation or for any public meeting exhibition or entertainment or for the manufacture consumption or sale of beer wine or spirituous liquors or as an hotel club billiards saloon dance hall sex shop funfair or amusement arcade or. for the purpose of any betting transaction within the meaning of the Betting Gaming and Lotteries Act 1 963 with or between persons resorting to the. Premises

Not to do or permit or suffer to be done on the Premises or any part thereof anything which shall or may be or become or cause an annoyance nuisance damage inconvenience disturbance injury or danger to the Landlord or the owners' lessees or occupiers of any other premises in the neighbourhood or persons having business with them.

(27) To take all necessary steps to prevent and not to permit any new window light opening doorway path passage drain or other encroachment right or easement to be made or acquired in to against over or upon the Premises and in case any such window light opening doorway path passage drain or other encroachment shall be made or threatened or attempted to be made or any such right or easement shall be acquired or attempted or threatened to be acquired then forthwith to give notice in writing thereof to the Landlord and to do at the request of the Landlord at the cost of the Landlord all such things as may be required for the purpose of

preventing the making or continuance of such encroachment or the acquisition of such right or easement

(28)   Not to sell goods by auction or permit or suffer any sale by auction to be held within or upon the Premises and not to store keep place exhibit or expose for sale or suffer to be stored kept placed exhibited or exposed for sale any plant machinery equipment materials stores goods or articles whatsoever upon any pavement or forecourt in front of or upon any external part of the Premises

(29)   Not to assign mortgage charge underlet or part with or share the possession of or permit the occupation by a licensee of part only of the Premises nor (save by way of a permitted assignment or underlease) to part with or share the possession of or permit the occupation by a licensee of the whole of the Premises

(30)   Not to assign or underlet nor to permit any underlessee or sub-underlessee to assign or underlet the whole of the Premises save with the Landlord's previous consent in writing such consent not to be unreasonably withheld or granted subject to unreasonable conditions PROVIDED that such consent for an assignment of the Premises by the Tenant may: -

(a)   Be withheld in the circumstances (specified for the purposes of s 1 9 (1 A) of the Landlord & Tenant Act 1927) set out in part 1 of the Schedule or any of them and/or

(b)   Be granted subject to the conditions (specified for such purposes) set out in part 2 of the Schedule or any of them

(31)   Not to underlet the whole of the Premises in consideration of a payment of a capital sum or premium

(32) Not to underlet the whole of the Premises save by way of an underlease: -

(a) At the best rent at which the Premises might reasonably be expected at the time to be let for the term granted by such underlease with vacant possession in the open market without payment of a premium (the amount of such rent to be previously approved in writing by the Landlord) such approval not to be unreasonably withheld and in any event at a rent not less than the Rent

(b) Containing provisions for the review of the rent reserved by such underlease in an upward direction only to a full market rental without taking a fine or a premium at the like times and in the like manner as the times and manner specified in this lease for the review of the Rent

(c) Containing (if the underlessee shall be a private limited company) a joint and several covenant on the part of at least two of its directors officers or members or other persons of satisfactory standing reasonably approved by the Landlord as principal debtors and so that they shall not be released even if the Tenant gives the company extra time to comply with any obligation or does not insist on its strict terms that: -

(i) the company will pay the Rent and observe and perform the covenants on the part of the underlessee contained in such underlease

(ii) they will indemnify the Tenant against any loss resulting from a default by the company and

if the underlease is disclaimed on the insolvency of the company they will if the Tenant so requires jointly take a new underlease of

the Premises at their own expense on the same terms and conditions as the terms and
condition of this underlease at the date of the disclaimer for a term equal to the remainder of the term thereby granted unexpired at such date

(d) Containing covenants identical to the covenants contained in sub-clauses (29) (30) {3 1) and (32) of this clause and a condition for re-entry on breach of covenant on the part of the underlessee and

(e) Otherwise in such form and containing such additional covenants and conditions and provisions as the Landlord shall reasonably and previously approve in writing

(33) On the grant of any permitted underlease or sub-underlease to obtain if the Landlord shall so require at the Tenant's expense an unqualified covenant in such document and form as the Landlord shall require on the part of the underlessee or sub-underlessee directly with the Landlord to observe and perform all the covenants on the part of the Tenant contained in this lease save for the covenants relating to the Rent and (if the intended underlessee or sub-underlessee shall be a private limited company) a joint and several covenant on the part of at least two of its directors officers or members or other persons of satisfactory standing approved by the Landlord directly with the Landlord as principal debtors and so that they shall not be released even if the Landlord gives the company extra time to comply with any obligation or does not insist on its strict terms that

(a) The company will observe and perform such covenant and

(b) They will indemnify the Landlord against any loss resulting from a default by the company

(34)	To give or cause to be given notice in writing of every assignment mortgage charge assent transfer underlease sub-underlease assignment mortgage or charge of an underlease or sub-underlease or devolution of or relating to the Premises and to deliver or cause to be delivered a certified copy of such instrument or any probate or letters of administration in any way relating to the Premises within 28 days after its execution or grant to the Landlord's solicitors and to pay a registration fee of £20.00 or such higher fee as such solicitors may reasonably require

(35)	Not without the Landlord's consent in writing such consent not to be unreasonably withheld to erect affix or exhibit or permit to be erected affixed or exhibited to or on any part of the exterior of the Premises or in or upon the windows of the Premises any aerial advertisement sign fascia placard bill notice signboard poster or other notification whatsoever and on the expiration or sooner determination of the Term to remove or efface any such aerial advertisement sign fascia placard bill notice signboard poster or notification and to make good any damage caused by such removal or effacement to the reasonable satisfaction of the Landlord

(36)	Not to form any permanent refuse dump or rubbish or scrap heap on the Premises or in or on any adjacent yard passageway or vacant land but to remove all refuse rubbish and scrap which may have accumulated on the Premises not less frequently than once a week

(37)	To clean the windows in the Premises as often as occasion shall require and at least once in every calendar month

(38)	To insure and keep insured any plate glass windows and doors in the Premises against damage or breakage to their full replacement value in the joint names of the Landlord and the Tenant with some reputable insurance office to be approved in writing from time to time by the Landlord (such approval not to be unreasonably withheld) and whenever so required to produce to the Landlord the policy and the receipt for the last premium payable for such insurance and in the case of damage to or destruction of such plate glass windows and doors to secure that all monies payable under or by virtue of the policy for such insurance shall be with all convenient speed laid out and applied in reinstating such plate glass windows and doors with glass of the same nature quality and thickness as at present and in case such monies shall be insufficient for such purpose to make good the deficiency

(39)   Not to give any bill of sale or other preferential security on the goods and chattels of the Tenant which shall for the time being be in or about the Premises

To produce to the Landlord from time to time such plans documents and other evidence as the Landlord may reasonably require in order to satisfy himself that the covenants on the part of the Tenant contained in this lease have been fully performed and observed.

4.   THE Landlord COVENANTS with the Tenant: -

(1)   That the Tenant paying the Rent and observing and performing the covenants on his part contained in this lease shall and may quietly enjoy the Premises during the Term without any interruption by the Landlord or persons lawfully claiming under the Landlord

(2)   (a)   To insure the Premises and the Landlord's fixtures and fittings therein of an insurable nature in such sum as the Landlord shall in his absolute discretion consider to be the costs likely to be incurred in rebuilding or reinstating the Premises at the time when such rebuilding or reinstatement is likely to take place having regard to all relevant circumstances including expected increases in building costs against loss or damage caused by the Insured Risks including the cost of shoring up

demolition and debris removal and architects' and other fees relating to the reinstatement of the Premises or such higher sum as the Tenant shall in writing require in an insurance office of repute

(b)   From time to time at the request and cost of the Tenant to provide the Tenant with full details of such policy or policies of insurance effected by the Landlord and evidence of payment of the current premium or premiums

(c)   In case of destruction or damage of or to the Premises or any such fixture or fitting by any of the Insured Risks (unless payment of any money payable under any policy for such insurance shall be refused either in whole or in part by reason of any act neglect or default of the Tenant or any sub-tenant or any servant agent or licensee of the Tenant or any sub-tenant) to secure that all monies payable under or by virtue of any such policy of insurance (other than money received in respect of loss of rent or professional fees as aforesaid) shall be with all convenient speed laid out and applied in rebuilding repairing replacing or otherwise reinstating the Premises or such fixture or fitting

5.   PROVIDED ALWAYS AND IT IS HEREBY AGREED that: -

(1)   If at any time during the Term any instalment of the Rent shall not be paid within 21 days after becoming due (whether lawfully demanded or not) or if any covenant on the Tenant's part contained in this lease shall not be performed or observed or if the Tenant or any surety for the Tenant shall compound or arrange with his creditors or suffer any distress or execution to be levied on the Premises or the contents thereof or (being an individual) shall commit any act of bankruptcy or enter into a voluntary arrangement within the meaning of section 1 of the Insolvency Act 1 986 or (being a company) shall

go into liquidation either compulsory or voluntary (except for a voluntary liquidation of a solvent company for the purpose of reconstruction or amalgamation) or if a receiver shall be appointed of its undertaking or an administration order is made under the Insolvency Act 1 986 or if the Premises shall be left vacant for a period of three months or more then and in any such case the Landlord or any person or persons duly authorised by the Landlord shall be entitled to re-enter into or upon the Premises or any part of the Premises in the name of the whole and to repossess and enjoy the Premises as if this lease had not been granted and thereupon the Term shall absolutely cease and determine without prejudice to any right of action or remedy of the Landlord in respect of any antecedent breach by the Tenant of any of the covenants contained in this lease

(2)   In the event of the destruction of or damage to the Premises by any of the Insured Risks so as to render the Premises or any part of the Premises unfit for occupation and use by the Tenant **PROVIDED THAT** and to the extent that the policy or policies of insurance effected by the Landlord shall not have been vitiated or payment of the policy monies refused in whole or in part as a result of any act neglect or default of the Tenant or any sub-tenant or any licensee servant or agent of the Tenant or any sub-tenant the Rent or a fair proportion of the Rent according to the nature and extent of the damage sustained shall be suspended until the Premises are rebuilt or reinstated fit for occupation and use or until the expiry of a period of three years from the date of the event causing such destruction or damage whichever shall be the earlier

(3)   If at any time during the Term any instalment of the Rent or any other money which may become payable by the Tenant (other than money payable under clause 6 (3) (b) of this lease and actually paid within 21 days of the date upon which it becomes due) to the Landlord under any of the provisions of this lease at any time or times shall not be paid on the due date

(whether such rent or other money has been formally or legally demanded or not) or shall be tendered but declined by the Landlord so as not to waive a breach of covenant then the amount for the time being unpaid shall (without prejudice to the Landlord's right of re-entry or any other right or remedy of the Landlord) as from such date or (in the case of money payable under clause 6 (3) (b) of this lease) as from a day 21 days after such date until paid bear and carry interest and the Tenant accordingly COVENANTS with the Landlord that in such circumstances and during such period or periods the Tenant will pay to the Landlord interest (as well after as before any judgment) on any such unpaid amount at the rate of £4.00 per cent per annum above National Westminster Bank PLC base rate for the time being prevailing or £10.00 per cent per annum whichever shall be the higher

(4)   All sums reserved or payable by the Tenant under this lease during the Term whether by way of reimbursement to the Landlord or otherwise shall be exclusive of value added tax and if value added tax or any other tax shall be or become payable on or in respect of any such sum such tax shall be paid or reimbursed by the Tenant in addition to the sum on or in respect of which such tax is payable

(5)   If at the expiration or sooner determination of the Term any fixture machinery plant or chattel belonging to the Tenant shall be left in the Premises by the Tenant for more than seven days the Landlord shall have power to sell the same as agent for and on behalf of the Tenant the money thereby arising (but not any interest thereon) less the costs of the sale and any money owing to the Landlord under any of the provisions of this lease or otherwise to be paid or accounted for by the Landlord to the Tenant on demand

(6)   Subject to the provisions of section 38 (2) the Tenant shall not on quitting the Premises be entitled to any compensation under sections 37 and 59 of the Landlord and Tenant Act 1954

(7)   Any notice under this lease shall be in writing and may be served on the person on whom it is to be served either personally or by leaving it for him at the Premises (if served upon the Tenant) or at his registered office (if a company) or last known place of business or abode or by sending it by registered post or the recorded delivery service to the Premises (if served upon the Tenant) or to such office or place and in the case of a notice to be served on the Landlord it may be served in like manner upon any agent for the Landlord duly authorized in that behalf PROVIDED ALWAYS that any notice addressed to "the Landlord" or "the Tenant" and served in accordance with the provisions of this sub-clause shall be deemed valid notwithstanding that it did not give the name of the Landlord or Tenant as the case may be

(8)   If the Tenant shall desire to determine the Term on either of the Review Dates and of such desire shall give to the Landlord not less than 6 months previous notice in writing specifying the desired termination date and if on the date so specified the Rent shall have been paid and the covenants and conditions on the part of the Tenant contained in this lease shall have been substantially observed and performed then on the date so specified the Term shall be determined and his lease shall cease to have effect without prejudice to any outstanding claims by either party against the other in respect of any antecedent breach of covenant

6.   (1)   IN this clause

(a) The expression "the Relevant Review Date" shall mean whichever one of the Review Dates may from time to time give rise to a review of the Rent under the provisions of this clause and the expression "the Relevant Review Period" shall mean the period from that date to the next of the Review Dates or (if the Relevant Review Date shall be the last of the Review Dates) to the end of the Term as the case may be

The expression "the Market Rent" shall mean the best yearly rent at which the Premises might reasonably be expected on the Relevant Review Date to be let as a whole with vacant possession in the open market by a willing landlord to a willing tenant for the Permitted Use and without payment of a premium for a term of equal length to the then unexpired residue length of the Term commencing on the Relevant Review Date under a lease containing the same terms and conditions (other than the initial amount of the Rent but including provisions identical to the provisions of this clause for the review of the rent thereby reserved at intervals of the same frequency from the commencement of such term as the frequency of the Review Dates) in all other respects as are contained in this lease as from time to time varied extended or rectified on the assumption (if not a fact) that at the Relevant Review Date

(I) all the covenants on the part of the Tenant contained in this lease as to repair and otherwise have been fully observed and performed at that date and

(ii) if the Premises have been damaged or destroyed that they have been fully restored and

(iii) the Premises are fit for and capable of immediate and full occupation and use and

(iv) no work has been carried out to the Premises by the Tenant which has diminished the rental value of the Premises and there being disregarded (so far as may be permitted by law)

(i) any effect on rent of the fact that the Tenant has been in occupation of the Premises and

(ii) any goodwill attached or attributable to the Premises by reason of any trade or business carried on by the Tenant and

(iii) any increase in rental value attributable to improvements (shown to be such by the Tenant) made to the Premises by and at the expense of the Tenant within the period of 21 years prior to the Relevant Review Date with the prior written consent of the Landlord other than in pursuance of an obligation on the part of the Tenant and

(iv) any Enactment restricting the amount of the yearly rent which the Landlord may lawfully demand or receive or which the Tenant may lawfully pay

(c) The expression "the Referee" shall mean an independent Chartered Surveyor experienced in the letting and valuation of property used for the Permitted Use who shall be appointed either by agreement between the parties by a date one month prior to the Relevant Review Date or one month after such date as the parties may agree under sub-clause (4) of this clause whichever shall be the later or in the absence of such agreement on the application of either party by the President for the time being of the Royal Institution of Chartered Surveyors or some other officer of that body if the President be unable to act

(2) Before on or after the Review Date or each of the Review Dates the Rent shall be reviewed and the Rent in respect of the Relevant Review Period shall be either the Rent payable immediately prior to the Relevant Review Date or the Market Rent whichever shall be the higher

(3) If for any reason whatever the Rent in respect of the Relevant Review Period shall not have been ascertained by the date of its commencement then

(a) The Tenant shall pay on account rent at the rate payable immediately prior to the Relevant Review Date until the Rent in respect of the Relevant Review Period shall have been ascertained and
b) If following such ascertainment the Rent in respect of the Relevant Review Period shall be greater than the Rent payable immediately prior to the Relevant Review Date the Tenant will within 7 days after ascertainment of the Rent in respect of the Relevant Review Period pay to the Landlord a sum equivalent to the Rent in respect of the Relevant Review Period as so ascertained from the commencement thereof to the next usual quarter day after the date of such ascertainment less all sums so paid on account together with interest at the rate of £2.00 per cent above National Westminster Bank PLC base rate from time to time on such sum from the Relevant Review Date until the date of actual payment or the date 21 days after the Rent in respect of the Relevant Review Period shall have been ascertained whichever shall be the earlier together with any further interest payable under clause 5 (3) of this lease

(4) The amount of the Market Rent at the Relevant Review Date shall in default of agreement between the Landlord and the Tenant by a date two months prior to the Relevant Review Date (or such later date as they may agree) be determined by the Referee who shall act as an expert and not as an arbitrator

(5) In addition to the determination of the Market Rent the award of the Referee may also contain directions as to the share in which the expense of the determination (including the expense of the appointment of the Referee) shall be borne and if

such award shall contain such directions then such expense shall be borne in such shares but otherwise such expense shall be borne by the Landlord and the Tenant in equal shares and the Landlord and the Tenant mutually covenant the one with the other to pay their respective shares of such expense accordingly

(6) The provisions of this clause shall apply notwithstanding any failure of either party to take or any delay by either party in taking any step leading to the agreement or determination of the Market Rent and time shall not be deemed to be of the essence of this clause

(7) (a) If at any time during the Term the amount of the Rent is in any way restricted by any Enactment so as to be irrecoverable in part then the maximum amount

from time to time permitted to be recovered shall be recoverable in lieu of the Rent until such restriction shall cease.

(b) As soon as such restriction shall cease the full amount of the Rent shall forthwith become payable and the difference between the full amount of the Rent and the amount recoverable prior to the cessation of such restriction proportionate to the period from such cessation to the next subsequent quarter day shall be payable within seven days of such cessation

(c) Within seven days of such cessation the Tenant will pay to the Landlord so far as permitted by law the difference between the Rent and the amount actually paid by the Tenant while such restriction was in force

THE SCHEDULE
PART I

Circumstances in which the Landlord's consent for an assignment of the Premises by the Tenant may be withheld.

1. That there are outstanding unpaid monies due from the Tenant to the Landlord under this lease or any deed supplemental to this lease

2. That there is (in the reasonable opinion of the Landlord) a material outstanding breach of the covenants on the part of the Tenant contained in this lease

PART 2

Conditions subject to which the Landlord's consent for an assignment of the Premises by the Tenant may be granted.

1. That on or before the assignment the Tenant enters into an agreement with the Landlord under which the Tenant: -

(a) guarantees the performance by the proposed assignee only whilst the assignee is the lessee under this lease of all the covenants on the part of the Tenant contained in this lease

(b) is liable to the Landlord as a principal debtor only whilst the assignee is the lessee under this lease and is not released even if the Landlord gives the proposed assignee extra time to comply with any obligation arising under this lease or does not insist on its strict terms and

(c) agrees that in the event that this lease is disclaimed the Tenant will accept the grant of a new tenancy of the Premises for a term expiring on the date on which the Term would have expired if this lease had not been disclaimed and on the same terms and conditions as the terms and conditions of this Lease at the date of disclaimer

PROVIDED that such agreement shall not impose on the Tenant any liability in relation to any time after the proposed assignee is released from the covenants on the part of the Tenant contained in this lease by virtue of the Landlord and Tenant (Covenants) Act 1995

2. That in the case of an assignment to a private limited company at least two of its directors officers or members or other persons of satisfactory standing to be approved by the Landlord (such approval not to be unreasonably withheld) shall covenant with the Landlord in such document and form as the Landlord shall reasonably require as principal debtors and so that they shall not be released even if the Landlord gives the company extra time to comply with any obligation arising under this lease or does not insist on its strict terms that

(a) the company will pay the Rent and observe and perform the covenants on the part of the Tenant contained in this lease

(b) they will indemnify the Landlord against any loss resulting from a default by the company and

(c) if this lease is disclaimed on the insolvency of the company they will if the Landlord so requires jointly take a new lease of the Premises at the expense of such person on the same terms and conditions as the terms and condition of this lease at the date of the disclaimer for a term equal to the remainder of the term unexpired at such date

SIGNED AND DELIVERED   )

REPAIRS - THE SCHEDULE

Main Roof Externally:

1.   The flat crown roof to the main roof structure is covered by felt and chippings and in good order. The mansard slate roof slopes have been re- slated and are in good order.

2.   The asphalt valley gutter has been repaired and is in good order.

Back Addition Lean-To Roof Slope:
3.   The back addition lean—to roof slope has been re-slated and is in good order.

Asphalt Roof over Shop Area:
4.   The asphalt roof has been repaired; minor ridging visible.

External Main Walls:

5.   New steel restraining straps (2 no.) fixed to front elevation around bay window structure.

6.   Cracking in the rear elevation above the lean—to roof slope has been cut out and repaired.

7.   Render repairs made to side elevation at ground level where former opening existed.

8.   Portico over Baker Street entrance repaired and in sound condition.

9.   Cracking to the end of the shop front at parapet level to Baker Street side repaired.

Rainwater Goods:

10. All rainwater goods replaced with PVC guttering and downpipes.

Chimney Stack:

11.. Defective rendering to chimney stack hacked off and repaired.

External Joinery:

12. New shop front window frames installed.
13. New Shop entrance door and frame installed.
14. Windows to all elevations in reasonable condition.

External Decorations:

15. External decorations are in good order.

INTERNALLY:

Second Floor West Bedroom:

16. The ceilings and walls in good order. Redecorated.
17. Skirtings, architraves and doors in reasonable condition. Paintwork in good order.

Second Floor East Facing Bedroom:

18. Ceilings and walls in good order. Redecorated.
19. Skirtings, architraves and doors paintwork in good order.

Bathroom:
20. Ceilings and walls in good order. Glazed tiling in fair condition.

21. New gas water heater fitted.
22. Sanitaryware reasonable.
23. Ceiling, walls and joinery redecorated.

Staircase:

24. Ceilings and walls redecorated and in good order. Minor defects to lining papers beneath the decorations.

First Floor Main East Room:

25. Ceiling and walls in good order. Redecorated.

26. Skirting, architraves and door in fair condition, repainted.

Kitchen:

27. Ceiling and walls in good order, redecorated.
28. A new sink unit, base unit with worktop and two double cupboard wall units fitted.

29. Glazed tiled splashback in good order.
30. Skirtings, architraves and door in good order, repainted.

W.C.

31. Ceilings and walls in good order. Redecorated.
32. New W.C. installed.

Ground Floor South Entrance Lobby:

33. Ceiling and walls in reasonable condition, redecorated.
34. Front door repaired, redecorated, fair condition.
35. Doors to basement, staircase and shop in good order, skirtings, architraves reasonable. All joinery repainted.

Back Addition Ground Floor Main Room:

36.   Ceiling fair, **walls repaired.** Basic condition, no decorations.

Rear Passage, Store and W.C.

37.   Ceiling repaired, walls repaired, basic condition, no decoration.
<u>Cloakroom</u>.

38.   ceiling repaired, walls repaired, fair condition, no decoration.
39.   Sanitaryware reasonable.

<u>Electrics</u>:

40.   Property rewired, in good order.

<u>Shop</u>:

41..   Shop ceiling, walls in good order.
42.   Decorations in good order.